Job Interview Questior

MW00848777

ADVANCED C++
INTERVIEW QUESTIONS
YOU'LL MOST LIKELY BE ASKED

349
Interview Questions

VIBRANT
PUBLISHERS

Advanced C++

Interview Questions
You'll Most Likely Be Asked

© 2021, By Vibrant Publishers, USA. All rights reserved. No part of this publication may be reproduced or distributed in any form or by any means, or stored in a database or retrieval system, without the prior permission of the publisher.

ISBN-10: 1-946383-70-8
ISBN-13: 978-1-946383-70-9

Library of Congress Control Number: 2012909253

This publication is designed to provide accurate and authoritative information in regard to the subject matter covered. The author has made every effort in the preparation of this book to ensure the accuracy of the information. However, information in this book is sold without warranty either expressed or implied. The Author or the Publisher will not be liable for any damages caused or alleged to be caused either directly or indirectly by this book.

Vibrant Publishers books are available at special quantity discount for sales promotions, or for use in corporate training programs. For more information please write to **bulkorders@vibrantpublishers.com**

Please email feedback / corrections (technical, grammatical or spelling) to **spellerrors@vibrantpublishers.com**

To access the complete catalogue of Vibrant Publishers, visit **www.vibrantpublishers.com**

Table of Contents

Dear Reader,

Thank you for purchasing **Advanced C++ Interview Questions You'll Most Likely Be Asked.** We are committed to publishing books that are content-rich, concise and approachable enabling more readers to read and make the fullest use of them. We hope this book provides the most enriching learning experience as you prepare for your interview.

Should you have any questions or suggestions, feel free to email us at **reachus@vibrantpublishers.com**

Thanks again for your purchase. Good luck with your interview!

- Vibrant Publishers Team

Advanced **C++** Interview Questions

Review these typical interview questions and think about how you would answer them. Read the answers listed; you will find best possible answers along with strategies and suggestions.

This page is intentionally left blank

Chapter 1

General Concepts

1: Explain Shallow Copy and Deep Copy in C++.

Answer:

When you use the assignment operator to copy an object or array into another, you are actually only copying the pointer of the first object into the other. This is shallow copy. A shallow copy passes on the reference to an object instead of the value stored in it. So when one of the object's value changes, the change reflects in both, rendering the copy of no use.

Deep copy is when the values are copied instead of the pointer that addresses the object or array. This is done by using an explicit copy constructor. When you use the assignment operator with a complex data type or object, it does only shallow copy.

2: Explain Volatile and Mutable.

Answer:

The *Mutable* keyword lets you change the value of a constant variable declared using the keyword const. Suppose you have a class and you have declared an object of that class as a const. Usually the const members are not allowed to be changed, unless the member is declared as mutable. The mutable members of a const class can be modified.

The *Volatile* keyword specifies that the value of the variable may be changed and hence reminds the processor to read or write the value every time it is being used. Volatile variables are not optimized because they should be ready to hold a wide range of values anytime during the program.

3: Explain translation unit in C++.

Answer:

A Translation unit is a single file created to compile a program. It includes the source code, the header files as directed by the #include statements, and any other conditional pre-processing directive as mentioned in the program. If any other program file is accessed by the source code, that file is also included here. All these are made into a single file which is compiled into an executable program, a library or an object file.

4: What is the difference between Static and Extern in C++?

Answer:

Static variables retain the same value across multiple instantiations. If a class has a static variable with a value x, the value will remain the same across all objects of that class. You can access this variable directly using the class name without any object. A static variable can be used across the classes within a program.

The extern keyword is used to create global variables that have scope across programs.

5: What are the preprocessor directives?

Answer:

Preprocessor directives are messages to the preprocessor and are processed before the program is compiled. For example, #include<iostream> tells the C++ preprocessor to include the contents of the iostream header file.

6: What is binary scope resolution operator and why is it used?

Answer:

When a class member function or attribute is defined outside the class, the name of the member function in the function header is preceded by the class name and the binary scope resolution operator (::). Binary scope resolution operator 'ties' each member function or data member with the class definition.

7: What is wrong in the following assignment?

char choice;

choice = "y";

Answer:

Here "y" is a string literal, so cannot be assigned to the character variable 'choice'. The correct assignment should be:

char choice;

choice = 'y';

8: What is the difference between a variable and a literal?

Answer:

Variables represent storage locations in memory, whereas literals are constant values assigned to variables.

9: How many bytes would be required to store '\n'?

Answer:

1 byte.

10: Integer literals are expressed in decimal by default. How would you express a hexadecimal number?

Answer:

Hexadecimal numbers are expressed by placing 0x (zero-x) before them. For example, 0xD4.

11: What would be the output of the following program?

```
#include<iostream>
using namespace std;
int main()
{
    char letter;
    letter = 66;
    cout << letter << endl;
    return 0;
}
```

Answer:

B

12: What would be the output of the following program?

```
#include<iostream>
using namespace std;
int main()
{
    int i;
    float f;
    f = 8.9;
    i = f;
    cout << i << endl;
    return 0;
}
```

Answer:

8, when a floating point value is truncated, it is not rounded.

13: Does the size of a data type vary? Which operator could be used for determining the size of a data type on any machine?

Answer:

Yes, size of some data types may vary from machine to machine. This is one of the problems of portability. For example, int could be 2 bytes or 4 bytes. The size of operator provides the number of bytes of memory used by any data type or variable.

14: How would the number 7,900,000 be represented in E notation and in scientific notation?

Answer:

E notation: 7.9 x 106

Scientific notation: 7.9E6

15: Which of the following is not a valid C++ data type? Why?

a) **double**

b) **unsigned long**

c) **unsigned double**

d) **long double**

Answer:

C. There is no unsigned floating point data type, because the float, double and long double variables can store both positive and negative numbers.

16: What are the 'Associativities' of an operator? When does it become an important issue?

Answer:

An operator's associativity could be 'left to right' or 'right to left'. If two operators have same precedence, they work according to their associativity. For example, 18/9 * 5 will be treated as ((18/9) * 5).

17: Predict the output:

```
#include<iostream>
using namespace std;
int main()
{
```

```
    int exp;
    exp = (5 +16 ) % 2 – 1;
    cout << exp << endl;
    return 0;
}
```

Answer:

The output will be "0".

18: Predict the output:

```
#include<iostream>
using namespace std;
int main()
{
    int x = 20, y = 10, z = 30;
    double avg;
    avg = x + y + z / 3.0;
    cout << avg << endl;
    return 0;
}
```

Answer:

The output will be "40.0".

19: Explain the Operator precedence when you are working with different data types.

Answer:

When dealing with different data types, both will be converted to the higher-ranking data type first and then the operation will be carried out according to the usual precedence. The scope operator, postfix and prefix operators come before the pointers after which the arithmetic operators come. The scaling operators *, / and % are considered first after which the addition and subtraction operators come.

20: What would be the output of the following program? Why?

```
#include<iostream>
using namespace std;
int main()
{
    short x = 32767;
    cout << x << endl;
    x++;
    cout << x << endl;
    x--;
    cout << x << endl;
    return 0;
}
```

Answer:

32767

-32768

32767

The data type short can hold integer values from – 32768 to +32767. In the beginning, x is 32767. The expression x++ makes x overflow and its value is wrapped around to -32768. The expression x - - makes it underflow and again its value is wrapped around to 32767.

21: What is type casting? How is it achieved in C++?

Answer:

Type casting is the process of performing data type conversion manually. It is achieved by using the static_cast operator, with general format:

static_cast<data type> (value)

Example:

double n = 7.9;

int a;

a = static_cast<int>(n)

22: Do you think the following code will serve its purpose? Explain your answer.

```
#include<iostream>
using namespace std;
int main()
{
    int visitors, months;
    double visitors_per_month;
    cout << "\n How many visitors: ";
    cin >> visitors;
    cout << "\n How many months: ";
    cin >> months;
    visitors_per_month = static_cast<double>(visitors/months);
    cout << "\n Average visitors per month " <<
    visitors_per_month << endl;
    return 0;
}
```

Answer:

The code is intended to avoid the integer division as the result is double. But here, the division would be still an integer division. The type cast would avoid the integer division, if the expression is correctly changed to:

visitors_per_month = static_cast<double>(visitors)/months;

23: What is the purpose of the stream manipulator 'setw'? Which header file should be included for using the stream manipulators in the program?

Answer:

The stream manipulator 'setw' is used for specifying the minimum number of spaces used for printing each number.

For example:

int value = 79

cout << setw(5) << value;

// would print '   79'

24: Predict the output:

```
#include<iostream>
using namespace std;
int main()
{
    double d = 25.927;
    cout << setprecision(3) << d << endl;
    return 0;
}
```

Answer:

25.9

25: What is the purpose of the rand() function? Why is srand() used?

Answer:

The rand() function produces pseudorandom numbers. For example, the statements:

cout << rand() << endl;

cout << rand() << endl;

cout << rand() << endl;

It would generate three different numbers, but it would generate the same three numbers every time the program runs.

The srand() function randomizes the results of rand(). It takes a seed value. If the seed value is different every time the rand() is executed, then rand() would generate different random numbers every time the program runs.

26: Illustrate the use of srand() by providing few statements.

Answer:

unsigned seed = time(0);

srand(seed);

cout << rand() << endl;

27: How can you limit the value of random numbers generated in the range of 1 through 100?

Answer:

int y;

y = 1 + rand() % 100;

28: How will you get the content from the header?

Answer:

We can get the content from header using preprocessor directive (#). Before creating the executable part, this directive notifies the compiler to import the code from the header and provide access to the files mentioned in the header.

29: How does the statement "cout" works?

Answer:

On seeing "cout<<", compiler calls a function, passing the text given in the double quotes as argument. Then the text given in the double quotes gets printed as it is.

Example:

Cout<< "Great Day"; // Great Day

30: How will you prevent the console window from closing after it finished execution?

Answer:

The console window can be stopped from closing after execution by using get function in cin statement which gets input from the user. Usually the console window gets closed once it finished the execution. When the 'get function' is used, it waits for the user input to exit.

Example:

cin>>get();

31: What is called undeclared variable?

Answer:

When a variable is used to store a value before declaration, then the variable is called "undeclared variable" and it creates compile time error.

Example:

int a,b;

c=a+b; // c - undeclared variable

32: How does the function of "=" and "==" differ?

Answer:

a) "=": Used for assignment. Value on the right gets stored in the variable on the left side

b) "==": Used to compare the value for equivalence

Example:

int p,m,;

p=10;m=5; //Assignment

if(m==5) //Comparison

cout << "Equality Operator";

33: How much space will be occupied by the data types "char", "int", "double" and "float"?

Answer:

a) "char" - 1 byte

b) "int" - 4 bytes

c) "double" - 8 bytes

d) "float" - 4 bytes

34: How do the local and global variables differs in scope?

Answer:

a) **Local variable:** One that is declared and used within a block/function. i.e. its scope is within the block/function

b) **Global variable:** Declared before or after the function/block and used anywhere in the program. i.e. its scope is within the program

35: What are the ways to initialize the variables?

Answer:

a) Using the assignment operator (normal initialization)

Example:

int p=18;

b) Using constructor

Example:

int p(18);

36: What is the purpose of "wide character"?

Answer:

Wide character is used to represent characters that differ from the normal characters i.e. its size is greater than normal "8 bit" characters.

37: What is the use of "define preprocessor"?

Answer:

Define preprocessor is used to define a constant value.

Example:

#define my_identifier my_value - #define state 99

Whenever the 'my_identifier' is used in the code, it gets replaced with the 'my_value'

38: What are the ways to define a constant in C++?

Answer:

In C++, a constant can be defined-

a) using 'const' keyword.

Example:

const my_type my_id =my_value; - const int state=99;

my_type - data type

my_id - identifier name

b) Using 'define preprocessor'

Example:

#define my_identifier my_value - #define state 99

39: What is the purpose of comma (,) operator in C++?

Answer:

The comma operator separates the expressions and after evaluation of expressions assigns the value available in the rightmost of "," to the identifier on the left side.

Example:

p = (m = 9, m + 1);

Assigns the value '9' to m and then assigns 9+1(10) to the identifier "p".

40: What is the output of the expression "3 + 8 / 4"? 5 or 2.6?

Answer:

The output is 5. According to operator precedence, "/" has higher precedence than "+". So, (8/4) get executed first, then 3 will be added.

i.e. $3 + (8 / 4)$

41: How are the I/O operations performed in C++?

Answer:

The I/O operations in C++ are performed using Streams. Insertion/Extraction of characters by a program to/from an object called Streams. The "iostream" header file contains this object. The "cin" is used with extraction operator ">>" for Input, and cout is used with insertion operator "<<"for output.

Example:

cin>>p;

cout<< "helllo";

42: How do you get a string as input?

Answer:

To get a string as input, we can use "cin". It gets the characters/single word. To get a sentence as string "getline" is used with cin. Because when cin is used, it stops getting the input once it finds the blank space.

Example:

cin>>my_strg;

string my_sentence1;

getline(cin,my_sentence1);

43: What are the two error streams in C++ and what is the difference between them?

Answer:

The error streams in C++ are clog and cerr. Both are connected to the "standard error" device and display the content.

a) clog object is 'buffered'. i.e. insertion at the clog gets buffered till it is filled or it displays

b) cerr object is 'unbuffered'. i.e. insertion at the cerr object, is directly displayed without buffering

This page is intentionally left blank

Chapter **2**

Control Statements and Decision Making

44: How do you write an infinite loop in C++ using the for statement?

Answer:

There are many ways in which you can use the for loop in C++ to write an infinite loop. The simplest way is to include a condition which will always be satisfied. Conditions like 2>1 will always be true so if such conditions are used in the for statement, it becomes an infinite loop. But this is not advised as it affects the readability. Instead, an empty for statement such as for (;;) is ideal for infinite loop. When you specify for (;;), there's no counter, condition or iterator. It is advisable to use an interrupt or exit statement in infinite loops else it will affect your system's functioning.

45: Assuming x = 20, y = 15; what would be the value stored in 'a' after the following statement is executed:

int a;

    a = x >= y;

Answer:

The value stored in 'a' will be 1.

46: Predict the output:

#include<iostream>

using namespace std;

int main()

{

    int x = 3, y = 7;

    cout << "x = " << x << "\n" << "y = " << y << endl;

    if (x > y);

    cout << "x is greater than y" << endl;

    return 0;

}

Answer:

x = 3

y = 7

x is greater than y

47: Predict the output:

#include<iostream>

using namespace std;

```
int main()
{
    int x = 7;
    if (x = 2)
        cout << "\n x = " << x << endl;
    return 0;
}
```

Answer:

x = 2

48: Write an 'if' statement that checks the value of variable 'age' to determine whether it is in the range of 18 through 65 and displays 'Acceptable age', when the condition is fulfilled.

Answer:

if (age >= 18 && age <= 65)

cout << "\n Acceptable age\n ";

49: When do you use a conditional operator (?:) ?

Answer:

The conditional operator (?:) is used for creating short expressions that work like a simple if-else statement.

50: Write a statement using conditional operator that assigns 0 to x, if y is greater than 10, otherwise assigns 1 to x.

Answer:

x = (y > 10)?0:1;

51: Rewrite the following expression, using an if-else statement: sum += a == 1? y : a*y;

Answer:

if(a == 1)

    Sum = sum + y;

else

    Sum = sum + a * y;

52: Can you change the following if-else statement block into a switch statement?

int a, b, c;

float x, y;

if(x == 0.5)

    y = a * x;

else if(x == 0.7)

    y = b * x;

else if(x == 0.9)

    y = c * x;

else

    y = x;

Answer:

No. The switch statement cannot test the value of a floating point literal. It only tests values of integer expression or literals. They also test character literal because, character literals are treated as integers.

53: Predict the output:

```
#include<iostream>
using namespace std;
int main()
{
int x = 5;
    cout << x << endl;
    cout << x++ << endl;
    cout << x << endl;
    cout << ++x << endl;
    return 0;
}
```

Answer:

5

5

6

7

54: Predict the output:

```
#include<iostream>
using namespace std;
int main()
{
    int x = 0;
    if(x++)
        cout << "It is true\n";
    else
```

```
        cout << "It is false\n";
    return 0;
}
```

Answer:

It is false.

55: Predict the output:

```cpp
#include<iostream>
using namespace std;
int main()
{
    int count = 0;
    while( count <10);
    {
        cout << count << endl;
        count++;
    }
    return 0;
}
```

Answer:

There will be no output. The program will create an infinite loop.

56: Convert the following if-else statement into a conditional expression:

```cpp
if (marks >= 50)
    cout << "Passed";
```

else

    cout << "Failed";

Answer:

cout << (marks >= 50 ? "Passed" : "Failed");

57: Write a for-loop statement that will print the numbers 1 through 10, but skip the number 5.

Answer:

```
for( int count = 1; count <= 10; count++)
{
    if ( count == 5)
        continue;
    cout << count << " ";
}
```

58: A program asks for a number in the range of 1 through 100. Write a simple while loop for input validation.

Answer:

```
while(number < 1 || number> 100)
{
cout << "\n Value outside range\n";
cout << "\n Please enter a number 1 - 100\n";
cin >> number;
}
```

This page is intentionally left blank

Chapter **3**

Functions and Recursion

59: What's wrong with the following function?

```
void display ( string m)
{
    cout << "\n Inside display\n" << m << endl;
    return 0;
}
```

Answer:

It is a void function, trying to return 0, an integer.

60: What is a function prototype? Write a prototype for a function add (), which takes the reference to two integer variables and returns another integer.

Answer:

A function prototype, also called 'Function declaration', is a way of providing information to the compiler about the function. It contains the function's return type, number of parameters and types of each parameter.

For example, prototype for function add () :

int add (int&, int&)

61: What is the difference between a local variable and a global variable?

Answer:

A local variable is defined inside a function and accessible only within the function.

A global variable is defined outside all functions and accessible to all the functions within the scope of the program.

62: Why global variables should not be preferred?

Answer:

Any statement in any function within the scope of the program may change the global variables of the program wrongly, which makes debugging difficult. Redesigning of any function that is dependent upon the global variable becomes more complex. For larger programs, presence of global variables makes it hard to understand.

63: What is a global constant?

Answer:

A global constant is a named constant available to all the functions in a program. Its value cannot be changed during the program execution.

64: What are the five storage class specifiers in C++?

Answer:

Five storage specifiers in C++ are: auto, register, extern, mutable, and static.

65: What does the function fmod (x, y) return?

Answer:

The function fmod(x, y) returns the remainder of x/y as a floating point number. For example, fmod(2.7, 1.2) will return 0.3.

66: What is the difference between the function ceil(x) and the function floor(x)?

Answer:

The function ceil(x) rounds x to the smallest integer not less than x; for example, ceil(7.3) is 8.0.

The function floor(x) rounds x to the largest integer not greater than x; for example, floor(7.3) is 7.0.

67: Predict the output:

```
#include<iostream>
using namespace std;
void displayStatic();
int main()
{
```

```cpp
    int count = 0;
    for(count = 0; count < 5; count++)
        displayStatic();
    return 0;
}
void displayStatic()
{
    static int s = 1;
    cout << s << endl;
    s++;
}
```

Answer:

1

2

3

4

5

68: Predict the output:

```cpp
#include<iostream>
using namespace std;
void doubleNum(int &);
int main()
{
    int a = 5;
    cout << a << endl;
```

```
    doubleNum(a);
    cout << a << endl;
    doubleNum(a);
    cout << a << endl;
    return 0;
}
void doubleNum(int & n)
{
    n *= 2;
}
```

Answer:

5

10

20

69: Is it right to call the function doubleNum of the last question as -- doubleNum(a + 5) ?

Answer:

No. Only variable can be passed by reference, not expressions.

70: What is function overloading?

Answer:

C++ enables defining several functions with the same name, as long as they have different signature. This is called function overloading.

71: Can the overloaded function have different return types?

Answer:

Yes, the overloaded functions can have different return types, when they have different parameter lists.

72: What is a function template? How do you define a function template?

Answer:

A function template is a model definition of a function, in which the program logic and operations are identical for all data types. Function template definitions begin with the keyword template, followed by a template parameter list enclosed in angle brackets (< and >).

For example:

```
Template <class T>
T add( T num1, T num2)
{
    Return num1 + num2;
}
```

73: What is a 'stub'? What is a 'driver'? When are they used?

Answer:

A stub is a dummy function that is called instead of the actual function it represents.

A driver is a program that tests a function by calling it. It passes the required arguments, if any, to the function and displays the return value(s), if any.

These functions are used in debugging.

74: What does the following function achieve?

```
unsigned long f(unsigned long n)
{
    If ((n==0) || (n==1))
    return n;
    else
    return f(n-1) + f(n-2);
}
```

Answer:

It returns the nth Fibonacci number.

This page is intentionally left blank

Chapter **4**

Arrays and Vectors

75: How much memory should be occupied by the array: char array [25]?

Answer:

25 bytes.

76: What's wrong with the following code snippet?

const int SIZE = 5;

int array[SIZE];

for(int count = 0; count <= SIZE; count++)

array[count] = 5;

Answer:

The program will write beyond the boundary of the array. It

would be logic error not a syntax error.

77: Is the following array initialization valid?

int array[5] = { 1, 2, ,4 , 5};

Answer:

No. If an element is left uninitialized, then all the elements following it should be uninitialized as well.

78: Is it possible to define an array without specifying its size?

Answer:

Yes, it is possible to define an array without specifying its size, as long as an initialization list is provided.

For example,

int numList[ ] = { 1, 2, 3 ,4 , 5};

79: What would be printed?

int array[ ] = { 2, 6, 8, 10};

cout << ++array[0];

Answer:

3

80: How can you prevent a function to modify the contents of an array that is passed to it as an argument?

Answer:

To prevent a function from making changes to the array elements, the const keyword should be used in the parameter declaration.

81: How do you define a vector?

Answer:

A vector can be defined to store any data type using a declaration like:

vector<type>name(size)

82: Which header file needs to be included to use vectors in your program?

Answer:

The vector header file.

83: Define a vector of 10 integers.

Answer:

vector<int>numbers(10);

84: Can you initialize the elements of a vector while defining?

Answer:

Yes, while specifying the starting size of a vector, an initialization value could be specified, which is copied to each element.

For example,

vector<int>numbers(10, 5);

85: Is it possible to initialize a vector with another vector without element-wise assignment? Is it possible to do the same with an array?

Answer:

Yes, a vector could be initialized with the values in another vector.

For example,

vector<int>numbers2(numbers);

The elements of the vector numbers will be copied to numbers2. It is not possible to do the same with an array. In case of an array an element to element assignment would be required.

86: What happens when you add a value to a vector that is already full?

Answer:

The vector automatically increases its size to accommodate the new value.

87: What is wrong with the following assignment?

vector<float>amounts;

amounts[0] = 7.3;

Answer:

The array subscript operator [ ] can be used to store values in an element of a vector that already exists. To store a value in a vector that does not have a starting size, the push_back() member function of the vector class is used. The correct statement here would be: amounts.push_back(7.3);

88: How can you determine the size of a vector?

Answer:

The size of a vector is obtained by using the size member function. For example,

int n = amounts.size();

89: How do you remove the last element from a vector?

Answer:

The last element of a vector can be removed by using the pop_back() member function . For example,

amounts.pop_back();

90: How can you clear the contents of a vector completely?

Answer:

The contents of a vector can be cleared of all its elements by using the member function clear (). For example,

amounts.clear();

91: What is the purpose of the vector member function empty() ?

Answer:

The member function empty() return true if the vector is empty and false if the vector has elements in it.

92: How do you retrieve a value stored at a particular element in the vector?

Answer:

To retrieve a value stored at a particular element in the vector, the member function at() is used. It returns the value of the element located at the specified position. For example,

float x = amounts.at(2);

This page is intentionally left blank

Chapter **5**

Pointers

_____

93: Can you use "delete this"?

Answer:

Even though "delete this" is a valid statement it should not be used due to the following reasons:

   a) The delete operator works only with objects that are created with the new operator. So if this object was not created using a new operator, you will not be able to use delete this.

   b) After using delete this you cannot access any member of this class.

Due to such complications in using delete with this it is advised not to use delete this, even though it can be valid in many cases.

94: What are pointers?

Answer:

Pointers are variables that contain memory addresses of other variables.

95: Predict the output:

```
#include<iostream>
using namespace std;
int main()
{
    int *ptr;
    int x = 14;
    ptr = &x;
    cout << *ptr << endl;
    *ptr++;
    cout << x << endl;
    return 0;
}
```

Answer:

14

15

96: Predict the output:

```
#include<iostream>
using namespace std;
int main()
{
```

```
    int array[] = {10, 20, 30, 40, 50};
    cout << *array << endl;
    return 0;
}
```

Answer:

10

97: Predict the output:

```
#include<iostream>
using namespace std;
int main()
{
    int array[] = {10, 20, 30, 40, 50};
    int *ptr;
    ptr = array;
    for(int c = 0; c<5; c++)
    cout << ptr[c] << " ";
    return 0;
}
```

Answer:

10 20 30 40 50

98: Predict the output:

```
#include<iostream>
using namespace std;
int main()
```

```
{
    int array[] = {10, 20, 30, 40, 50};
    int *ptr;
    ptr = array;
    for(int c = 0; c < 5; c++)
    {
        cout << *ptr << " ";
        ptr++;
    }
    return 0;
}
```

Answer:

10 20 30 40 50

99: Is it possible to compare pointers using the C++ relational operators?

Answer:

Yes, pointers can be compared by using any of C++ relational operators: >, <, ==, !=, >=, <=.

100: What is the difference between pointers to constant data and constant pointers?

Answer:

A pointer to a constant, points to a constant item. The data that the pointer points to cannot change, but the pointer itself can change. With constant pointers, it is the pointer itself that is constant. Once the pointer is initialized to with an address, it cannot point to another address.

101: Why could you declare a pointer parameter as a constant pointer?

Answer:

A constant pointer will protect against writing code in the function that may accidentally change the argument and also the function will be able to accept the addresses of both constant and non constant arguments.

102: What is the purpose of the new operator?

Answer:

The new operator is used to dynamically allocate memory.

103: What is the purpose of the delete operator?

Answer:

The delete operator is used to free the memory that has been dynamically allocated with the new operator.

104: What is a function pointer?

Answer:

It is a pointer to a function, i.e., the address where the code for the function resides.

105: Declare a function pointer that will take two integer parameter and return a Boolean value.

Answer:

bool (*fptr)(int, int);

This page is intentionally left blank

Chapter 6

Control Structures, Array and Pointers

106: What are the control statements used in C++?

Answer:

a) **'if' statement:** checks the condition, if true that block gets executed

b) **switch:** executes the statement that matches with the specified input

c) **'for' loop:** performs conditional checking and incrementation

d) **'while' loop:** checks the condition, if satisfied that block gets executed

e) **do.while:** block gets executed first and the condition is checked for remaining iteration

107: What is the function of continue and break?

Answer:

a) When 'continue' is encountered, the control exits the current block and continues the loop as usual

b) When 'break' is encountered, the control exits from the loop

108: What will happen if you pass a variable var1 as an argument to a function(arg1) from main() and make changes to the variable within the called function ?

Answer:

a) When the variable is passed normally, changes in one function will not reflect in another function

b) However, when a variable is passed as reference, the changes will reflect in another function

109: Give an example for normal function call and call by reference.

Answer:

Normal Function:

```
int fctn1 (int p){
    return p+10;
}
main(){
int a=10;
int b= fctn1(a);
```

cout<< b; //20

}

Call by Reference:

void fctn1 (int &p){

    p += 10;

}

main(){

int a=10;

fctn1(a);

cout<< a; //20

}

110: How will you assign a default value for last parameter in a function?

Answer:

When a function is called with all the parameters, default value is ignored. If the last argument is not passed during a function call, default value is taken.

Example:

int f1(int m,int n=9){

    return m+n;

}

void main(){

    int b=f1(5, 3); //8

      (or)

    Int b=f1(1); //10 - (takes default value)

111: How will you store the elements of the same type in a continuous memory location?

Answer:

This can be done using Array which stores the elements of the same type in continuous location starting from 0.

Example:

int arr_var[4]= {3, 5, 9, 8 };

112: How much memory space will be allocated for the array of integer type with length 4?

Answer:

a) Integer takes memory of 2 bytes

b) Length of the array is 4, so memory occupied by the array will be 8 bytes

113: How will you display the output with a particular space to be filled by specified amount?

Answer:

The output can be displayed using setfill function that is available in the "iomanip" header file.

Example:

cout<< setfill(7);

cout<< "Hello"; //*******Hello (fill up to the length 7)

114: How will you get the address of an array variable?

Answer:

The address of an array variable can be obtained using pointer.

Example:

int p[3]={1, 3, 5}; //array

int *a; //creation of pointer variable

a=p; //assigning address of first array element

cout<< "Second Value:" << *(a+1); //Second Value:3

115: What are the ways of passing an array as an argument?

Answer:

Following are the ways of passing an array as an argument:

  a) **Using sized array** - functn(int p,int a[5]);
  b) **Using unsized array** - functn(int p,int a[]);
  c) **Using pointer** - functn(int p,int *a);

116: How will you return an array from a "function"?

Answer:

An array can be returned from a function using pointer. A function returning array should be declared as returning pointer.

Example:

```
int *functn(){
...
}
main(){
int *a;
a=functn();
...
}
```

117: How will you notify the end of the value in an array?

Answer:

The end of the value can be notified using "null space". Memory will be allocated to the length specified in the declaration of an array. But the input value may be lesser than the specified length. Hence "\0" is used to indicate the end of the sequence.

Example:

char my_var1[]={'s', 't' , 'y' , 'l' , 'e' , '\0'};

118: What are the ways to create an array with null-terminated sequence of characters?

Answer:

Using '\0'

    char my_var1[]={'s', 't' , 'y' , 'l' , 'e' , '\0'};

Using double quotes(" ")

    Char my_var1[]= "style";

119: How will you convert the char array into a string?

Answer:

The char array can be converted into a string using "assignment operator".

Example:

char my_var1= "style";

string my_var2;

my_var2=my_var1;

120: How will you get the address of a variable?

Answer:

The address of a variable can be obtained using 'reference operator'(&). On declaring a variable, memory needed for that variable will be allocated with respect to its length. Address of memory is randomly assigned by the operating system at run time.

Example:

int p=989;

int q=&p; //address of p gets stored in q

121: What is the purpose of "Dereference operator"?

Answer:

Dereference operator is used to access the value stored in the address which is assigned to the pointer.

Example:

int p=989;

int q=&p; //address of p gets stored in q

int m=*q; //value of p gets stored in m

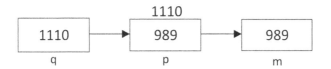

122: How will you assign a value to a variable using pointer?

Answer:

int my_val1, my_val2;

int *my_ptr1;

my_ptr1 = &my_val1; //my_ptr1=address of my_val1

*my_ptr1 = 778; //assign 778 to its reference i.e)my_val1=778

cout<< "value_1"<< my_val1; //778

my_ptr1 = &my_val2; //my_ptr2=address of my_val2

*my_ptr1 = 333; //assign 333 to its reference i.e)my_val2=333

cout<< "value_2"<< my_val2; //333

123: How much space will be occupied by the pointer of type int, char and double?

Answer:

The data type of each pointer may differ, but the memory allocation (same number of bytes) will be same for each pointer. However the memory differs in case of normal variable.

Example:

int m; double p; //'m' takes 2 bytes and 'p' takes 8 byte

int *q; double *n; //both 'q' and 'n' occupies same byte

124: What is the difference between "k2=k1" and "*k1=*k2"?

Answer:

int *k1,*k2; //pointer variable

*k1=*k2 - Assigns the value pointed by 'k2' to the variable pointed by k1

k2=k1 - value of k2 is assigned to k1

125: What is the relationship between array and pointers?

Answer:

The identifier of an array contains the address of its first element.

So address can be assigned to a pointer variable without using ampersand(&) symbol. Array is a 'constant pointer'.

Example:

int myvalues[]={1,2,9};

int *k;

k = myvalues; //address of first array element gets stored in k

126: Will it be possible to assign a pointer to a array identifier?

Answer:

No. Array is a 'constant pointer'. So it is not possible to assign any value to a constants.

Example:

int myvalues[]={1,2,9};

int *k;

k = myvalues; //this assignment is possible

myvalues=k; //not possible

127: What is the meaning of the statement (const char *myvar1= "Status")?

Answer:

Declaration of pointer variable ('myvar1') and initialization of contents to which the pointer is pointing.

Example:

Here the variable 'myvar1' contains the address of the first character "S".

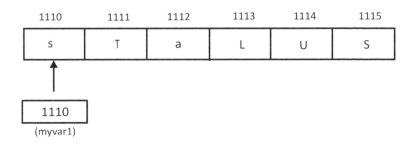

128: Is the following assignment possible?

const char *myvar1;

myvar1= "Status";

cout << myvar1;

Answer:

Yes. myvar1 is not constant, only the value at myvar1 is constant. So it can be assigned after declaration.

129: What is the function of " *k++ " and " (*k)++ " ?

Answer:

a) *k++ - '++' has higher precedence than '*'. Hence 'k' gets incremented and points to the next element and returns the value pointed by 'k' before incrementation

b) (*k)++ - Value pointed by 'k' is incremented

130: What is the output of following code?

int aa=10; //&aa=1111

int *k;

int **r;

k=&aa; //&k=2222

r=&k;

cout << "Single pointer:" << *k<<endl;

cout << "Double pointer:" << **r;

Answer:

Output:

Single pointer: 10

Double pointer: 10

131: How will you use the pointer with no data type?

Answer:

This can be done using void pointer. It points to the data that has no data type. Type casting can be used to convert to the required data type.

Example:

```
int add1(void * aa, int bb){
    int *aptr;
    aptr = (int*)aa;
    return (*aptr+bb);
    }
main(){
    int a1=10, b=20;
    int *myptr;
    myptr=&a1;
    int res= add1(&a1,b);
    cout << res;
    }
```

132: What is called 'Null pointer'?

Answer:

When the value pointed by the pointer is null, it is called null pointer.

Example:

int *myptr=NULL;

cout << myptr; //0

133: How will you pass a function as argument to another function using pointer?

Answer:

Pointer should be created to a function which needs to be passed as an argument.

Example:

```
void display(int k){
    cout << k;
}
void input(int n, int (*ptr_val) (int)){
    int nn=n*n
    (*ptr_val)(nn);
}
void main(){
    int m=10;
    int (*ptr_int) (inta) = display;
    input(m,ptr_int);
}
```

134: How will you allocate memory for a variable dynamically?

Answer:

This can be done using new operator. It allocates the memory and returns the pointer to the first element.

Ptr_var = new data_type; - dynamically allocates memory for single element of specified data type

Ptr_var = new data_type[7]; - dynamically allocates memory for 7 elements of specified data type

135: What are the ways to check the successful allocation of memory?

Answer:

a) **Using 'nothrow'.** When the allocation fails, 'Null pointer' will be returned by the new operator and the execution of program will continue

   Example:

   ptr_var = new (nothrow)int[3];

b) **Using Exceptions.** When the allocation fails, it throws 'bad_alloc' exception. Execution of the program stops, when the exceptions are not handled by the handler specified. This is the default method used by the new operator

136: How will you use delete operator?

Answer:

The delete operator is used to clear the dynamically allocated memory. There are two ways to use delete operator:

delete ptr_var; - single element's memory will be deleted

delete [] ptr_var; - deletes the array element's memory

137: Consider three variables of data type int, float and string. How will you store these values in a contiguous memory location?

Answer:

It can be done using 'Structure'.

Example:

```
struct my_var{
    int number;
    float nn;
    string name;
}obj1;
My_var obj2;
```

138: How will you access the value pointed by the pointer in structure?

Answer:

The value can be accessed using '->' operator.

Example:

```
struct my_var{
    int number;
    string name;
}obj1;
Main(){
    int q=99;
    my_var *ptr_var;
    ptr_var = & obj1;
    ptr_var -> number = q;
```

cout << obj1.number; // 99

139: How will you use your own type name for data types?

Answer:

This can be done using 'typedef'. It uses the user defined data type for the variable. User defined type is based on existing data type.

Example:

typedef int user_integer ;

user_integer xx=899;

This page is intentionally left blank

Chapter **7**

Object Oriented Programming and Classes

140: When do you need a Copy Constructor?

Answer:

If you have not explicitly defined a constructor, when you create a new object, the default copy constructor will be called. But the default copy constructor will only perform a shallow copy. It will never do a deep copy. A shallow copy is fine if your class does not have pointers. But you need a deep copy, if you are using pointers in your class. That's exactly when you need an explicit copy constructor too.

141: Which of the following two statements call copy constructor and which one calls assignment operator?

MyCopyClass mccO1, mccO2;

MyCopyClass mccO3 = mccO1; // (1)

mccO2 = mccO1; // (2)

Answer:

The statement *MyCopyClass mccO3 = mccO1;* calls a copy constructor since the object mccO3 is initialized as a copy of another object mccO1 of the same class.

The statement *mccO2 = mccO1;* is using a simple assignment operator as the object mccO2 is already initialized and it is only assigned the values of mccO1.

142: What are Virtual functions?

Answer:

Virtual functions are function declarations that are provided in a class definition. They are not defined in the class, instead defined by the deriving class. Virtual functions provide a framework of the common functionalities expected of the base class. The derived classes can each define them in their own ways. If they are defined in the base class and the derived class does not override the function, it will not be functional for the derived class. That's why virtual functions are not defined in the base class and are left to the derived classes to override.

143: Can you define a Virtual Copy Constructor?

Answer:

The very basic rule about a constructor is that it cannot be declared as a virtual function. A constructor cannot be static also since you cannot call a constructor function as such. It is automatically called by the processor when a new object instance is created. Virtual constructor cannot be defined as if you are declaring a constructor; it has to be with the definition. But the functionality can be obtained by declaring a virtual function inside the class and calling it in the constructor.

144: What is an 'object' in object oriented programming?

Answer:

An object is a software entity that contains both data and the procedures. Data contained in an object are known as the attributes of the object and the procedures performed by the object are called its member function. In C++, an object is implemented by the class keyword.

145: What is 'encapsulation'?

Answer:

Encapsulation refers to the combining of data and function into a single object.

146: What is 'data hiding'?

Answer:

An object can hide its data from code outside the object. Only the member functions may directly access and make changes to the attributes. This is called 'data hiding'.

147: What is the default access of a class?

Answer:

Default access of a class is private.

148: When do you use the const keyword with member functions?

Answer:

When the function needs to be prevented from changing any data stored in the calling object, it is declared a constant function by writing the const keyword after the parentheses.

149: Can you declare constructors and destructors as const?

Answer:

No, constructors and destructors cannot be declared const.

150: What is a friend function? What are the friend classes?

Answer:

A friend function is a function that is defined outside the scope of a class, but still can access all the members of the class. A friend class is a class that can access all the members of another class.

151: Class A is a friend of class B. Can class B access the members of class A?

Answer:

No, class A being a friend class of class B, can access members of class B, but not vice versa. The friendship relation is neither symmetric nor transitive.

152: What is 'this' pointer?

Answer:

Every object has access to its own address through a pointer, which is called the 'this' pointer of the object.

153: The memory used up by *this* pointer is not counted in the size of the object. Why is it so?

Answer:

The *this* pointer is not a member of the object. It is only a pointer that points to the current instance of the object. It can be used to access the non-static members of the class. It is passed to the program as a hidden argument to all non-static functions of the class. The static functions and members do not require *this* pointer as they can be accessed without the instance of the class.

154: Can *friend* functions be overloaded?

Answer:

A *friend* function can access all public, private and protected members of a class. It can be accessed from outside the class without an instance. *Friend* functions can be overloaded too. You need to mention that the function is a friend in every overloaded version inside the class.

155: What are the static data members of a class?

Answer:

Generally each instance (also called object) of a class has its own copy of all members of the class. Static data members are data variables that are shared by all the instances of the class, not specific to any instance of the class.

156: Explain the *register* storage class.

Answer:

If you want your variable to be stored in the registry instead of

RAM, you have to declare it as a *register* variable. You can no longer point to it as it is not located in the memory and hence does not have a pointer. Variables such as counters can be declared as *register* variables. But that does not guarantee that the variable will be stored in the register. It depends upon the hardware and other implementations.

157: Do you agree with the statement:

The static member functions do not have a 'this' pointer. Why?

Answer:

Yes. Static data members and static member functions exist independent of any object of a class. So they don't need any 'this' pointer, which is object specific.

158: What is a constructor?

Answer:

A constructor is a member function that is automatically called when a class object is created.

159: What is a destructor?

Answer:

A destructor is a member function that is automatically called when an object is destroyed.

160: Predict the output:

```
#include<iostream>
using namespace std;
class demo
```

```cpp
{
    private:
    int val;
    public:
    demo()
    {
        val = 3;
        cout << val << endl;
    }
    demo(int x)
    {
        val = x;
        cout << val << endl;
    }

    ~demo()
    {
        cout << val << endl;
    }
};
int main()
{
    demo a, b(4), c(7);
    return 0;
}
```

Answer:

3

4

7

7

4

3

161: What is the difference between the 'Student' structure and the 'Student' class?

struct Student

{

    string name;

int age;

};

class Student

{

    string name;

    int age;

};

Answer:

The attributes of the structure 'Student' can be accessed from outside the structure. They have public access. But the attributes of the class 'Student' cannot be accessed outside the class scope.

162: Predict the output:

#include<iostream>

```
using namespace std;
class A
{
    static int a;

    public:
    A()
    {a++;}

    int geta() const
    { return a;}
};
int main()
{
    A a1, a2, a3;
    Cout << "We have " << a3.geta() << "objects\n";
    return 0;
}
```

Answer:

We have 3 objects

163: What is a copy constructor?

Answer:

A copy constructor is used when you want to create an object as a copy of another object of the same type with the values. Usually when you use the = operator, only the address of the object is copied to the new object. When this is not enough and you want to copy the values too, you need to use the copy constructor which explicitly copies the values of each member to the new object. So with a copy constructor, you can initialize an object of the same type and populate it with values from the source object. This can be used to pass parameters or return values of class functions.

164: Which operators cannot be overloaded?

Answer:

The following operators cannot be overloaded:

Conditional operator (?:), Dot operator (.), sizeof operator, binary scope resolution operator(::), .* operator.

165: How does C++ differentiate between overloaded postfix operators and prefix operators?

Answer:

The overloaded postfix operator function takes a dummy int parameter.

166: Consider the following class student:

class student

{

    string name;

    int no_of_tests;

    double marks;

...

};

Write a copy constructor for this class.

Answer:

```
student(const student &s)
{
    name = s.name;
    no_of_tests = s. no_of_tests;
    marks = new double[no_of_tests];
    for(int i = 0; i< no_of_tests; i++)
    marks[i] = s.marks[i];
}
```

167: Write a constructor for the class student described above, which will take two parameters, a string for name and an int for no_of_tests and assign a default score of 0.0 to all the tests.

Answer:

```
student(string n, int t)
    {
name = n;
        no_of_tests = t;
        marks = new double[t];
        for(int i = 0; i< t; i++)
        marks[i] = 0.0;
    }
```

168: Write a destructor for the class student described above.

Answer:

```
~student()
    {
```

Delete [] marks;

}

169: How do you overload an operator?

Answer:

An operator is overloaded by writing a non-static member function or non-member function definition in which the function name should be the keyword operator followed by the symbol of the operator.

170: Why should an overloaded operator always be a non-static function?

Answer:

An overloaded operator should always be a non-static function because these functions will be called on an object of the class and they should operate on that object.

171: Can you change the precedence and associativity of an operator by overloading it?

Answer:

No., we cannot change it.

172: Can you change the number of operands an operator works on by overloading it?

Answer:

No, we cannot change that.

173: Can you create a new operator by operator overloading?

Answer:

No, only existing operators could be overloaded, new operators cannot be created.

174: What is wrong with the statement?

int * ptr = new int[100];

delete ptr;

Answer:

The first statement creates an array of 100 integers and assigns the starting memory of the array to ptr. The array should be deleted entirely by the statement: delete [] ptr;

This page is intentionally left blank

Chapter **8**

Inheritance, Polymorphism and Virtual Functions

175: Explain Conditional Compilation.

Answer:

Conditional compilation lets you define what parts of your programs can be compiled and what parts need not. If you are writing generic code and want to compile it based on certain conditions, you can use conditional compilation. If you want to run the program in debug mode, you can use conditional compilation. You can also prevent a particular portion of code from compiling if you put it inside a false condition. The #if - #endif constructs are used for conditional compilation. These are pre-processor directives like #define and #include.

176: Explain when # is used and ## is used in C++.

Answer:

is used in C++ when you need to convert the token into a string with quotes. ## is used to concatenate two tokens. You can define a function using the #define directive which converts the given token into string using # as below:

#include <iostream>

using namespace std;

#define make_string(valx) #valx


```
int main () {
        cout << make_string (Learning C++) << endl;
        return 0;
}
```


This will result in Learning C++ as the output. When the pre-processor invokes make_string(Learning C++), it is instead converted into "Learning C++" which makes the statement cout << "Learning C++" << endl;

Similarly, the following program explains the use of ##

#include <iostream>

using namespace std;

#define add_strings(valx, valy) valx ## valy

```
int main () {
        int ab = 10;
        int cd = 20;
        int abcd = 235;
        cout << add_strings (ab,cd) << endl;
        return 0;
}
```

This will result in 235 as the output. When the pre-processor invokes add_strings(ab, cd), it returns abcd which makes the statement cout << abcd << endl;

177: What is inheritance?

Answer:

Inheritance is basically a form of software reuse. A new class is created that uses the capabilities of an existing class, customizes or enhances them. The existing class is called the base class and the new class is called the derived class. The derived class is said to be inherited from the base class.

178: Is it possible for a base class to call a member function of a derived class?

Answer:

No, inheritance does not work in reverse direction.

179: What is the basic difference between inheritance and composition?

Answer:

Inheritance follows a 'is-a' relationship, i.e., an object of a derived class can also be treated as an object of its base class; whereas, composition follows 'has-a' relationship where an object contains one or more objects of other classes as members.

180: Who can access the protected members of a base class?

Answer:

The members and friends of the base class and the members and friends of all derived classes of the base class, can access the members of the base class.

181: Can a derived class access the private members of the base class?

Answer:

No, private members of the base are inaccessible to the derived class.

182: What is the default access specification of a base class?

Answer:

Private.

183: Predict the output:

```
#include<iostream>
using namespace std;
class A
{
```

```
    public:
    A()
    {cout << "\n Base class Created";}
~A()
    {cout << "\n Base class Destroyed";}
};
class B
{
    public:
    B()
    {cout << "\n Derived class Created";}
~B()
    {cout << "\n Derived class Destroyed";}
};
int main()
{
    B a;
    cout << "\n Program end";
    return 0;
}
```

Answer:

Base class Created

Derived class Created

Program end

Derived class Destroyed

Base class Destroyed

184: What is polymorphism?

Answer:

Polymorphism lets you use the same functions in different ways. It also lets you define the same function in different ways to function differently each time. Function overriding lets you define the same function to do different types of processing depending on the object that is calling it. This is usually used in inheritance when the base class and derived class have the same function but different definitions in their respective classes. Function overloading and operator overloading lets you use the same function differently with different data types.

185: How is polymorphism implemented in C++?

Answer:

Polymorphism is implemented via virtual functions and dynamic binding.

186: What is the difference between redefining a base class function and overloading a base class function?

Answer:

When a derived class has a function with the same name as a base class's function, and the base class function is not virtual, it is said that the function is redefined in the derived class. If the base class's function is virtual, it is said that the function is overridden.

187: How is static binding different from dynamic binding?

Answer:

In static binding, the compiler knows clearly which function has to be called when there are multiple versions available. Overloaded functions follow static binding.

Dynamic binding happens when the function which is called is identified only during the run time, based on the object which is calling the function. Overridden functions are bound dynamically. This is also called late-binding or run-time binding. Inherited function calls or virtual function calls are bound dynamically.

188: Pointers to a base class may be assigned the address of a derived class object. Does it work in reverse?

Answer:

No. Pointer to a derived class object cannot be directly assigned the address of a base class object.

189: How can you make a derived class object pointer point to a base class object?

Answer:

This could be done by using a type cast. For example, say, aptr is an object is an object pointer of base class A and bptr is an object pointer of a class B, which derived from A.

Then, we can write,

A * aptr = new A();

B * bptr = static_cast< B *>(aptr);

190: When and why should you declare a destructor as virtual?

Answer:

When a class has the potential to become a base class, its destructor should be declared as virtual. This is done because, otherwise when a base class pointer or reference variable reference a derived class object, the derived class's own destructor won't be called (because of static binding), when the variable goes out of scope.

191: What is an abstract base class?

Answer:

An abstract base class is a generic class, which cannot be instantiated, but other classes are derived from it.

192: What is the characteristic of a pure virtual function?

Answer:

A pure virtual function is a virtual member function of a base class that must be overridden. When a class contains one or more virtual function(s), it becomes an abstract base class.

193: How do you declare a pure virtual function?

Answer:

A pure virtual function is declared by adding an equal sign followed by zero (= 0), after the closing brackets in the function definition.

For example, virtual void display() = 0;

194: What is wrong in the following code?

#include<iostream>

using namespace std;

class A

```
{
int a;
public:
    A()
    {a = 2;}
    A( int x)
    {a = x;}
    virtual void showdata() = 0;
};
class B: public A
{
    int b;
public:
    B()
    {b = 0;}
B( int y)
    {b = y;}
    Void showdata()
    {
        cout << a << endl;
        cout << a << endl;

};
int main()
{
    B m;
```

```
    m.showdata();

    return 0;

}
```

Answer:

Class B cannot access the private variable 'a' of class A. It should have had protected access specifier to be accessible to B.

195: What is multiple Inheritance?

Answer:

When a derived class has two or more bases classes, it is called multiple Inheritance.

196: We cannot instantiate objects of an abstract base class. Can we declare pointers to objects of an abstract class?

Answer:

Yes, we can declare pointers and references to objects of an abstract base class, which is used for enabling polymorphic use of objects instantiated from concrete derived classes.

197: What is the purpose of the dynamic_cast operator?

Answer:

The dynamic_cast operator checks the type of the object to which a pointer points, then determines whether the type has a relationship with the type to which the pointer is being converted. If so, dynamic_cast returns the object's address. If not, dynamic_cast returns 0.

198: What is the purpose of the typeid operator?

Answer:

The typeid operator returns a reference to a type_info object that contains information about the operand's type, including the type name. To use typeid, the program must include header file <typeinfo>.

199: What is the importance of the dynamic_cast and the typeid operators with respect to polymorphism?

Answer:

These operators are part of C++'s runtime type information (RTTI) feature, which allows a program to determine an object's type at runtime.

This page is intentionally left blank

Chapter **9**

Exceptions and Exception Handling

200: What is an exception?

Answer:

An exception is a value or an object that indicates an error.

201: What is the purpose of exception handling?

Answer:

Exception handling helps in creating programs that can resolve problems that occur at execution time. It allows programs to continue executing as if no problems had been encountered and informs the user about the problem before terminating in a controlled manner.

202: What is a 'try' block?

Answer:

The *try* block contains the program or statements that must be tried for errors or exceptions. All instructions or commands that may throw an exception are put under the *try* block. Any errors or exceptions raised during runtime are caught by the *catch* block and corresponding action is taken there. User-defined exceptions can also be *thrown* within the *try* block.

203: How are the exceptions caught?

Answer:

Exceptions are caught by catch handlers. At least one catch handler must immediately follow a try block. Each catch handler specifies an exception parameter that represents the type of exception the catch handler can process.

204: What is a 'throw point'?

Answer:

The point in the program at which an exception occurs is called the throw point.

205: What happens when an exception is caught?

Answer:

Whenever an exception is caught in the *try* block, the control moves on to the *catch* block where the corresponding exception is caught. Within the *catch* block, if the exact exception is not caught, the program stops abruptly. Hence a generic exception can be included as the last option in the *catch* block. This is because the *catch* block is executed sequentially till the first matching exception is encountered.

206: What is 'rethrowing' an exception?

Answer:

With nested *try* blocks, it is sometimes necessary for an inner exception handler to pass an exception to an outer exception handler. Sometimes, both an inner and an outer *catch* block must perform operations when a particular exception is thrown. These situations require that the inner *catch* block rethrow the exception so the outer *catch* block may catch it. A *catch* block can rethrow an exception with the throw; statement.

207: What do you mean by 'unwinding the stack' in reference with exception handling?

Answer:

The function executing a throw statement will immediately terminate. If that function was called by another function, and the exception is not caught, then the calling function will terminate as well. This process is known as unwinding the stack.

208: What happens if the *new* operator fails?

Answer:

When the operator *new* fails, it throws an exception bad_alloc, which is defined in the new header file.

209: What is an exception specification?

Answer:

An exception specification enumerates a list of exceptions that a function can throw. A function can throw only exceptions of the types indicated by the exception specification or exceptions of any type derived from these types. If the function throws any other type of exception, function unexpected is called and the program terminates.

210: What happens when a function does not have an exception specification?

Answer:

A function with no exception specification can throw any exception.

Chapter **10**

Class Template and Standard Template Library (STL)

211: Explain Signal Handling.

Answer:

Signals are like errors that interrupt the normal running of a program. You may not be able to capture and handle all signals raised by a program. But there are a few which can be caught and handled within the program such as SIGILL which stands for illegal instruction and SIGSEGV for invalid storage access. Unexpected events can be trapped using the signal function. Signal handling is like exception handling but in signal handling the external interrupts are captured instead of the errors raised by the program.

212: How are STL and Object Class Library related?

Answer:

The Standard Template Library provides C++ the fundamental functionalities for developers in terms of containers, algorithms and iterators. These three complete the basic requirements of C++ framework and lets the developer create Business Intelligence applications using it. The STL is a simple and extensible framework which is but obsolete now and instead the Standard Function Library comes of use. The Object Class Library contains a collection of classes and objects that form the basis of object oriented programming in C++. The STL is now a part of the Object Class Library.

213: What is a class template?

Answer:

A class template is used to create generic classes and abstract data types. Class templates allow the programmer to create a general version of a class without having to duplicate code to handle multiple data types.

214: What does the Standard Template Library contain?

Answer:

STL contains many templates for useful data structures and algorithms.

215: What are the most important data structures defined in STL?

Answer:

Containers and Iterators.

216: What is a container?

Answer:

A container is a class that stores and organizes data. For example, vector, deque, list, set, map etc.

217: What is an iterator?

Answer:

An iterator is an object that helps in accessing the data elements in a container. It acts like a pointer. Iterators are associated with the container.

218: What is the difference between a sequential container and an associative container?

Answer:

A sequential container like list or vector, allows sequential access of data elements, whereas, the associative container uses keys to rapidly access elements.

219: What are the sequential containers present in STL?

Answer:

Vector, deque, and list

220: What are the associative containers present in STL?

Answer:

Set, multiset, map and multimap

221: What is the difference between the set and multiset data structures?

Answer:

Both the data structures store a set of keys. The set data structure does not allow duplicate values but the multiset data structure allows duplicate values.

222: What is the difference between map and multimap data structures?

Answer:

Both the data structures map a set of keys to data elements. The map data structure allows only one key per data but the multimap data structure allows many keys per data.

223: Assume that you have a vector object 'vect' of integers. Write a for loop to access its elements using an iterator.

Answer:

```
vector <int> vect;
vector<int> :: iterator iter;
...
for(iter = vect.begin(); iter < vect.end(); iter++)
cout << *iter << endl;
```

224: Which algorithm randomly shuffles the elements in a container?

Answer:

The random_shuffle function rearranges the elements randomly.

For example,

random_shuffle((vect.begin(), vect.end());

This page is intentionally left blank

Chapter **11**

Functions, Class and Template

225: What is the way to bind the functions and variables in a single structure?

Answer:

The functions and variables can be bound in a single structure using 'class'. Functions and variables of the class can be accessed by creating an object for that class.

Example:

class my_cname{

class my_cname{

    int my_var1=99;

    public:

```
    void display(int p){
        cout << p;
}
}obj1;
main(){
obj1.display(5);
}
```

226: When a function or variable is defined with a private access specifier, what is the accessibility of that function?

Answer:

By default, all the functions and members are declared as private. They are:

a) Accessible within the same class and

b) From the their 'friend function'

227: How will you create a function definition of a class outside of that class?

Answer:

This can be done using the scope resolution operator and is treated like 'inline'

function.

```
class my_cname{
    public:
        void display(int);
} obj1;
void my_cname :: display (int p){
```

```
    cout << p;
}
```

228: How will you initialize an object?

Answer:

An object can be initialized using constructor. It also allocates a dynamic memory for an object during its creation.

Constructor function is called whenever an object is created.

Example:

```
class my_cname{
    public:
    my_name(int q){
            int m=q; }
void display(){
        cout << m; }
}
main(){
    my_cname.obj1(5);
    obj1.display(); }
```

229: How will you clear the dynamically allocated memory?

Answer:

We can clear dynamically allocated memory using delete function in destructor.

Example:

```
class my_cname{
        public:
```

```
       int *m;
       my_name(int q){
               m=new int;
               *m=q;}
       ~my_name(){
           delete m; }
       void display(){
           cout << *m; }
       }
   main(){
       my_cname.obj1(5);
       obj1.display(); }
```

230: Can a constructor be overloaded?

Answer:

Yes. Overloading of functions takes place when there is a same function with different arguments. During the declaration of object, corresponding overloaded function is called based on the arguments.

Example:

```
Class my_class{
    my_class(){
        cout << "Hellllo";
    }
    my_class(int a, int aa){
        int c = a + aa;
    }
```

```
}
main(){
    my_class obj1;
    my_class obj2(5,8);
}
```

231: How will you create an object to call a overloaded constructor function?

Answer:

It is like a normal variable declaration.

Example:

```
class_name objname(parameters);
```

The compiler calls the default constructor on the creation of an object. To call a default constructor function,

```
class_name objname;
```

232: How will you pass an object as argument to a function?

Answer:

This can be done using 'copy constructor'. Data of an object that is passed as an argument gets copied into the data member of the current object.

Example:

```
Class my_class{
        my_class(int a, int aa){
        int c = a + aa;
        }
        my_class(const my_class& rcvdobj){
```

```
                a = rcvdobj.a;
                b = rcvdobj.aa;
                c = rcvdobj.c;
        }
        }
main(){
        my_class obj2(5,8);
        my_class obj1(obj2);
}
```

233: Give an example for creating a pointer to class.

Answer:

```
class my_cname{
        public:
        void input(int q){
                int m=q; }
        void display(){
                cout << m; }
        }
main(){
        my_cname obj1,*bb,cc;
        obj1.input(3);
        bb= &cc;
        bb->input(7);
        cout << "obj1:" << obj1.display(); //obj1:3
        cout << "bb:" << bb->display(); // bb: 7

}
```

234: Give an example for polymorphism.

Answer:

```
class moprn{
    public:
    int a,b;
    void input(int aa,int bb){
        a=aa;b=bb;}
}
class moprn : public Addition{
    void result(){
        return (a+b);}
class moprn : public Subtraction{
    void result(){
        return (a-b);}
void main(){
    Addition ad;
    Subtraction su;
    moprn *mptr1= &ad, *mptr2=&su;
    mptr1 -> result(9,7); mptr2 -> result(9,7);
    cout << ad.result(); // 16
    cout << ad.result(); //2
}
```

235: What will happen if the super class function's access specifier is protected and you are trying to override this function in sub class with 'private' access specifier?

Answer:

It will give compilation error since the overriding function can give more access than overrided function, not less access. Hence protected can be overridden as public not private.

236: What will happen if the object of sub class is created and assigned to its super class reference variable as stated below?

```
class A{
    void display1(){
        cout << "Inside A"
    }
}
class B{
    void display2(){
        cout << "Inside B"
    }
}
void main(){
    A a= new B();
    a.display2(); // Compile time error
}
```

Answer:

It gives compilation error since display2() is not defined in class A (superclass).

237: Give an example for function overriding.

Answer:

The functions of super class can be overridden in the sub class if any properties need to be modified.

Class Animal {

    Void sound() {

        s.o.p("...");

    }

    Void eat() {

        s.o.p("...");

    }

}

Class Cat extends Animal {

    Void sound() {

        s.o.p("...");

    }

    Void eat() {

        s.o.p("...");

    }

}

238: How will you overload an operator?

Answer:

An operator can be overloaded using 'operator' syntax.

Syntax:

my_type operator operator_symbol (my_params){..}

my_type - usually it is the class name

operator - operator to be overloaded

my_params - parameters for the function

239: How will you declare and initialize a static member?

Answer:

Static variables are similar to a global variable. This variable is common to all the objects of the class.

Declaration:

Normal variable declaration prefixed with 'static' keyword.

Eg.) static int my_var1;

Initialization:

Eg.)int class_name :: my_var1=5;

240: Consider a template class that contains one function. When an object of particular type is created, how will you implement the template that should contain different method?

Answer:

This can be done using 'Template Specialization'.

```
template <class T>
class my_temp {
T my_var1;
public:
    my_temp (T myarg1) { my_var1=myarg1;}
    T ndisplay () {
        cout << "Numbers" << endl;
        return my_var1;}
};


template <>
class my_temp <char> {
```

```
char my_var1;
public:
    my_temp (char myarg1) { my_var1= myarg1;}
    char cdisplay ()
    {
        cout << "Characters" << endl;
        return my_var1;
    }
};

void main () {
    my_temp <int> intvar (3);
    my_temp <char> charvar ('i');
    cout << myint.ndisplay() << endl; //3
    cout << mychar. cdisplay () << endl; //i
}
```

241: How will you access the variable declared inside the namespace?

Answer:

This can be done using 'scope resolution operator'.

```
namespace my_space1{
    int my_var1 = 11;
}
namespace my_space2{
    int my_var1 = 21;
}
```

```
void main(){
    cout << my_space1 :: my_var1; //11
    cout << my_space2 :: my_var1; //21
}
```

242: How will you the use the variable in namespace without using "::"?

Answer:

This can be done with the help of keyword 'using'. It takes the variable defined in 'using' into the current declarative region.

Example:

```
namespace my_space1{
    int my_var1 = 11;
}
namespace my_space2{
    int my_var1 = 21;
}
void main(){
    using my_space1 :: my_var1;
    cout << my_var1; //11
    cout << my_space2 :: my_var1; //21
}
```

243: What are the ways to do type casting?

Answer:

a) Using 'implicit' conversion.

Example:

int my_int = 33;

float my_flt ;

my_flt = mt_int;

b) Using 'Explicit' conversion.

Example:

int my_int = 33;

float my_flt ;

my_flt = (float)mt_int;

244: How will you use an existing file for an output operation?

Answer:

This can be done using 'ios::trunc'. If an existing file is opened for an output operation, old content will be deleted and replaced with the new output.

Example:

my_newfile.open("abg.bin", ios::trunk);

This page is intentionally left blank

Chapter **12**

Stream Input Output

245: C++ offers type-safe I/O – explain.

Answer:

In C++, I/O operations are executed in a type-sensitive way. If an I/O member function has been defined to handle a particular data type, then that member function is called to handle that data type. If the compiler finds no match between the type of the actual data and a function for handling that data type, it generates an error.

246: How can you use the stream insertion operator (<<) and the stream extraction operator (>>) on user-defined data type?

Answer:

We can use them by overloading the << and >> operators.

247: How can the stream extraction operator >> and the stream insertion operator << work upon all types of data?

Answer:

The >> operator is overloaded to input data items of fundamental types, strings and pointer values. Similarly, the << operator is overloaded to output data items of fundamental types, strings and pointer values.

248: How can you change the base in which integers output?

Answer:

The stream manipulator hex sets the base to hexadecimal (base 16) and oct sets the base to octal (base 8). The manipulator dec resets the base to decimal.

249: Predict the output:

```
#include<iostream>
#include <iomanip>
using namespace std;
int main()
{
    int number = 20;
        cout << number << endl;
        cout << hex << number << endl;
        cout << dec << number << endl;
    return 0;
}
```

Answer:

20

14

18

250: What is the purpose of the stream manipulator *scientific*?

Answer:

It specifies output of a floating-point value in scientific notation.

251: What is the purpose of the stream manipulator *boolalpha*?

Answer:

It sets the output stream to display bool values as the strings "true" and "false".

This page is intentionally left blank

Chapter 13

File Processing

252: Which file access flag would you use if you want all output to be written to the end of an existing file?

Answer:

The ios::app access flag lets you read and write to the end of an existing file. ios::app moves to the end of file every time it is accessed. If you want to see and insert into a file, you must use ios::ate. But ios::app always points to the end of the stream.

253: What is the specialty of the fstream data type that the ifstream and ofstream data types do not have?

Answer:

The fstream data type allows both reading and writing, while the ifstream data type allows only for reading, and the ofstream data type allows only for writing.

254: Assume that the file info.txt already exists, and the following statement executes. What happens to the file?

fstream file("info.txt", ios::out);

Answer:

The file is truncated. Its contents are erased.

255: Should file stream objects be passed to functions by value or by reference? Why?

Answer:

File stream objects should be passed to functions by reference because the internal state of file stream objects changes with most every operation. They should always be passed to functions by reference to ensure internal consistency.

256: Explain ios::hardfail, the file stream object bit.

Answer:

The ios::hardfail is set to true when an irrecoverable error has occurred. This is different from reaching the end of file or eof which is checked with ios::eofbit, failure of an attempted operation which sets the ios::failbit to true and an invalid operation attempt which sets the ios::badbit. You can check it with the function fail() which returns true if the ios::hardfail or ios::failbit is true.

257: When is a file stream object's ios::eofbit bit set? Which

member function reports the state of this bit?

Answer:

It is set when the end of the file has been encountered. The eof member function reports the state of this bit.

258: How do you read the contents of a text file that contains whitespace characters as part of its data?

Answer:

The getline() function in the istream header lets you read the string line by line from file. In case you want, you can set other delimiters such as '>>' for white space. By default it is '\n' for new line which will help you read every line including the white spaces in it.

259: What are the arguments to be passed to a file stream object's write member function?

Answer:

The write function takes two arguments: The starting address of the section of memory that is to be written to the file, and the number of bytes that are to be written.

260: What are the arguments to be passed to a file stream object's read member function?

Answer:

The read function takes two arguments: The starting address of the section of memory where the data will be stored, and the number of bytes to read.

261: What type cast do you use to convert a pointer from one type to another?

Answer:

You can either use dynamic_cast or reinterpret_cast to explicitly typecast a pointer. While dynamic_cast sets some limitations on the typecasting, reinterpret_cast lets you convert even to totally unrelated object types. Dynamic_cast is used exclusively for pointers and object references. You can use it when you want to typecast a pointer of derived class to the base class. The other way would work only if the base class is polymorphic. Reinterpret_cast on the other hand lets you convert any pointer to any other type even if they are not related. No type-checking is done here on the value or the definition. But they end up being very system-specific and hence will not be portable.

262: What is the difference between the seekg and seekp member functions?

Answer:

The seekg function moves a file's write position, and the seekp function moves a file's read position.

263: How do you get the byte number of a file's current read position? How do you get the byte number of a file's current write position?

Answer:

The tellg member function provides the byte number of the current read position and the tellp member function gives the byte number of the current write position.

264: How do you determine the number of bytes that a file contains?

Answer:

First the seekg member function is used to move the read position to the last byte in the file. Then the tellg function is used to get the current byte number of the read position.

265: Write a statement that defines a file stream object named students. The object will be used for both output and input to and from a file.

Answer:

fstream students("students.txt", ios::in | ios::out);

266: Write a code snippet that defines a file stream object named employees. The file should be opened for both input and output in binary mode. If the file open operation fails, it should display an error message.

Answer:

fstream employees;

employees.open("emp.txt", ios::in | ios::out | ios::binary);

if (!employees)

cout << "Failed to open file.\n";

267: What does the following code achieve?

dataFile.seekg(0L, ios::end);

n = dataFile.tellg();

cout << n << " \n";

Answer:

It determines the number of bytes contained in the file associated with the file stream object dataFile.

268: The dataFile file stream object is used to sequentially access data. The program has already read to the end of the file. Write code that rewinds the file.

Answer:

dataFile.clear();

dataFile.seekg(0L, ios::beg);

Chapter **14**

Miscellaneous

269: Explain the ? : Operator.

Answer:

This is known as the ternary operator in C++. The ?: can be used instead of the if-else conditional statement. The ternary operator has the same precedence as the assignment operator. It can be used to simplify the conditional statement as in the given example:

int numb1 = 0;

int numb2 = 0;

(choicenum > 1 ? numb1 : numb2) = 1;

In the above piece of code, if the value of choicenum is greater than 1, then the value 1 is assigned to numb1. Otherwise, the value 1 is assigned to numb2.

270: Explain stack and heap in C++.

Answer:

Stacks and heaps are used for dynamic memory allocation in C++. Stack contains all the variables that are declared within a function. Heap contains the free memory area allocated to a program. The heap is used to allocate dynamic memory during the runtime. Whenever the program invokes the *new* operator, the free memory available in the heap is allocated for the object. Whenever a *delete* operator is called, the memory allocated in the heap gets free which is again available for allocation.

271: How is dynamic memory allocation done in C++ efficiently?

Answer:

Dynamic memory allocation is efficiently done in C++ using constructors and destructors. Whenever an object instance is created using the *new* operator, the user-defined or default constructor is called which allocates the memory for that instance of the object. Though an explicit destructor is rarely declared, when the program ends or the object becomes out of scope it is automatically destroyed by calling the default destructor. Otherwise whenever the *delete* operator is used, it calls the destructor and frees the memory allocated for the object.

272: Explain Multithreading in C++.

Answer:

Multithreading is a process in which two or more parts of the same program can be run concurrently as different threads. Every thread is a piece of program which can be run independently by a scheduler. When many threads run parallel, it makes the program more efficient. Even though C++ does not explicitly support multithreading, there are ways in which it can be achieved, making the most of what the OS supports. To create multi-threaded applications in C++, you must include the *thread* header file.

273: Explain CGI.

Answer:

CGI or Common Gateway Interface helps the scripts in the website communicate with the web servers. It is the standard for communication set by the NCSA which lets international gateways communicate efficiently with HTTP servers that contain information. CGI lets users run programs and scripts using a web browser instead of invoking websites or web pages. CGI programs or scripts can be written in C, C++, Python, Shell, PERL etc.

274: Why CGI is a better choice than other scripting languages?

Answer:

Many of the scripting languages that are commonly used such as Javascript, Java, ActiveX etc can be browser specific. They may not run on certain types of browsers or can be blocked by the browser or the security firewall. But CGI scripts are not dependent on the browser. CGI only acts as an interface which lets the user invoke programs written in other languages through the web browser. It only acts as an interactive gateway between HTTP and the programs.

This page is intentionally left blank

HR Questions

Review these typical interview questions and think about how you would answer them. Read the answers listed; you will find best possible answers along with strategies and suggestions.

1: Tell me about a time when you didn't meet a deadline.

Answer:

Ideally, this hasn't happened – but if it has, make sure you use a minor example to illustrate the situation, emphasize how long ago it happened, and be sure that you did as much as you could to ensure that the deadline was met. Additionally, be sure to include what you learned about managing time better or prioritizing tasks in order to meet all future deadlines.

2: How do you eliminate distractions while working?

Answer:

With the increase of technology and the ease of communication, new distractions arise every day. Your interviewer will want to see that you are still able to focus on work, and that your productivity has not been affected, by an example showing a routine you employ in order to stay on task.

3: Tell me about a time when you worked in a position with a weekly or monthly quota to meet. How often were you successful?

Answer:

Your numbers will speak for themselves, and you must answer this question honestly. If you were regularly met your quotas, be sure to highlight this in a confident manner and don't be shy in pointing out your strengths in this area. If your statistics are less than stellar, try to point out trends in which they increased toward the end of your employment, and show reflection as to ways you can improve in the future.

4: Tell me about a time when you met a tough deadline, and how you were able to complete it.

Answer:

Explain how you were able to prioritize tasks, or to delegate portions of an assignment to other team members, in order to deal with a tough deadline. It may be beneficial to specify why the deadline was tough – make sure it's clear that it was not a result of procrastination on your part. Finally, explain how you were able to successfully meet the deadline, and what it took to get there in the end.

5: How do you stay organized when you have multiple projects on your plate?

Answer:

The interviewer will be looking to see that you can manage your time and work well – and being able to handle multiple projects at once, and still giving each the attention it deserves, is a great mark of a worker's competence and efficiency. Go through a typical process of goal-setting and prioritizing, and explain the steps of these to the interviewer, so he or she can see how well you manage time.

6: How much time during your work day do you spend on "auto-pilot?"

Answer:

While you may wonder if the employer is looking to see how efficient you are with this question (for example, so good at your job that you don't have to think about it), but in almost every case, the employer wants to see that you're constantly thinking, analyzing, and processing what's going on in the workplace. Even if things are running smoothly, there's usually an opportunity somewhere to make things more efficient or to increase sales or productivity. Stress your dedication to ongoing development, and convey that being on "auto-pilot" is not conducive to that type of success.

7: How do you handle deadlines?

Answer:

The most important part of handling tough deadlines is to prioritize tasks and set goals for completion, as well as to delegate or eliminate unnecessary work. Lead the interviewer through a general scenario, and display your competency through your ability to organize and set priorities, and most importantly, remain calm.

8: Tell me about your personal problem-solving process.

Answer:

Your personal problem-solving process should include outlining the problem, coming up with possible ways to fix the problem, and setting a clear action plan that leads to resolution. Keep your answer brief and organized, and explain the steps in a concise, calm manner that shows you are level-headed even under stress.

9: What sort of things at work can make you stressed?

Answer:

As it's best to stay away from negatives, keep this answer brief and simple. While answering that nothing at work makes you stressed will not be very believable to the interviewer, keep your answer to one generic principle such as when members of a team don't keep their commitments, and then focus on a solution you generally employ to tackle that stress, such as having weekly status meetings or intermittent deadlines along the course of a project.

10: What do you look like when you are stressed about something? How do you solve it?

Answer:

This is a trick question – your interviewer wants to hear that you don't look any different when you're stressed, and that you don't allow negative emotions to interfere with your productivity. As far as how you solve your stress, it's best if you have a simple solution mastered, such as simply taking deep breaths and counting to 10 to bring yourself back to the task at hand.

11: Can you multi-task?

Answer:

Some people can, and some people can't. The most important part of multi-tasking is to keep a clear head at all times about what needs to be done, and what priority each task falls under. Explain how you evaluate tasks to determine priority, and how you manage your time in order to ensure that all are completed efficiently.

12: How many hours per week do you work?

Answer:

Many people get tricked by this question, thinking that answering more hours is better – however, this may cause an employer to wonder why you have to work so many hours in order to get the work done that other people can do in a shorter amount of time. Give a fair estimate of hours that it should take you to complete a job, and explain that you are also willing to work extra whenever needed.

13: How many times per day do you check your email?

Answer:

While an employer wants to see that you are plugged into modern technology, it is also important that the number of times you check your email per day is relatively low – perhaps two to three times per day (dependent on the specific field you're in). Checking email is often a great distraction in the workplace, and while it is important to remain connected, much correspondence can simply be handled together in the morning and afternoon.

14: What has been your biggest success?

Answer:

Your biggest success should be something that was especially meaningful to you, and that you can talk about passionately – your interviewer will be able to see this. Always have an answer prepared for this question, and be sure to explain how you achieved success, as well as what you learned from the experience.

15: What motivates you?

Answer:

It's best to focus on a key aspect of your work that you can target as a "driving force" behind your everyday work. Whether it's customer service, making a difference, or the chance to further your skills and gain experience, it's important that the interviewer can see the passion you hold for your career and the dedication you have to the position.

16: What do you do when you lose motivation?

Answer:

The best candidates will answer that they rarely lose motivation, because they already employ strategies to keep themselves inspired, and because they remain dedicated to their objectives. Additionally, you may impress the interviewer by explaining that you are motivated by achieving goals and advancing, so small successes are always a great way to regain momentum.

17: What do you like to do in your free time?

Answer:

What you do answer here is not nearly as important as what you don't answer – your interviewer does not want to hear that you like to drink, party, or revel in the nightlife. Instead, choose a few activities to focus on that are greater signs of stability and maturity, and that will not detract from your ability to show up to work and be productive, such as reading, cooking, or photography. This is also a great opportunity to show your interviewer that you are a well-rounded, interesting, and dynamic personality that they would be happy to hire.

18: What sets you apart from other workers?

Answer:

This question is a great opportunity to highlight the specific skill sets and passion you bring to the company that no one else can. If you can't outline exactly what sets you apart from other workers, how will the interviewer see it? Be prepared with a thorough outline of what you will bring to the table, in order to help the company achieve their goals.

19: Why are you the best candidate for that position?

Answer:

Have a brief response prepared in advance for this question, as this is another very common theme in interviews (variations of the question include: "Why should I hire you, above Candidate B?" and "What can you bring to our company that Candidate B cannot?"). Make sure that your statement does not sound rehearsed, and highlight your most unique qualities that show the interviewer why he or she must hire you above all the other candidates. Include specific details about your experience and special projects or recognition you've received that set you apart, and show your greatest passion, commitment, and enthusiasm for the position.

20: What does it take to be successful?

Answer:

Hard work, passion, motivation, and a dedication to learning – these are all potential answers to the ambiguous concept of success. It doesn't matter so much which of these values you choose as the primary means to success, or if you choose a combination of them. It is, however, absolutely key that whichever value you choose, you must clearly display in your attitude, experience, and goals.

21: What would be the biggest challenge in this position for you?

Answer:

Keep this answer positive, and remain focused on the opportunities for growth and learning that the position can provide. Be sure that no matter what the challenge is, it's obvious that you're ready and enthusiastic to tackle it, and that you have a full awareness of what it will take to get the job done.

22: Would you describe yourself as an introvert or an extrovert?

Answer:

There are beneficial qualities to each of these, and your answer may depend on what type of work you're involved in. However, a successful leader may be an introvert or extrovert, and similarly, solid team members may also be either. The important aspect of this question is to have the level of self-awareness required to accurately describe yourself.

23: What are some positive character traits that you don't possess?

Answer:

If an interviewer asks you a tough question about your weaknesses, or lack of positive traits, it's best to keep your answer light-hearted and simple – for instance, express your great confidence in your own abilities, followed by a (rather humble) admittance that you could occasionally do to be more humble.

24: What is the greatest lesson you've ever learned?

Answer:

While this is a very broad question, the interviewer will be more interested in hearing what kind of emphasis you place on this value. Your greatest lesson may tie in with something a mentor, parent, or professor once told you, or you may have gleaned it from a book written by a leading expert in your field. Regardless of what the lesson is, it is most important that you can offer an example of how you've incorporated it into your life.

25: Have you ever been in a situation where one of your strengths became a weakness in an alternate setting?

Answer:

It's important to show an awareness of yourself by having an answer for this question, but you want to make sure that the weakness is relatively minor, and that it would still remain a strength in most settings. For instance, you may be an avid reader who reads anything and everything you can find, but reading billboards while driving to work may be a dangerous idea.

26: Who has been the most influential person in your life?

Answer:

Give a specific example (and name) to the person who has influenced your life greatly, and offer a relevant anecdote about a meaningful exchange the two of you shared. It's great if their influence relates to your professional life, but this particular question opens up the possibility to discuss inspiration in your personal life as well. The interviewer wants to see that you're able to make strong connections with other individuals, and to work under the guiding influence of another person.

27: Do you consider yourself to be a "detailed" or "big picture" type of person?

Answer:

Both of these are great qualities, and it's best if you can incorporate each into your answer. Choose one as your primary type, and relate it to experience or specific items from your resume. Then, explain how the other type fits into your work as well.

28: What is your greatest fear?

Answer:

Disclosing your greatest fear openly and without embarrassment is a great way to show your confidence to an employer. Choose a fear that you are clearly doing work to combat, such as a fear of failure that will seem impossible to the interviewer for someone such as yourself, with such clear goals and actions plans outlined. As tempting as it may be to stick with an easy answer such as spiders, stay away from these, as they don't really tell the interviewer anything about yourself that's relevant.

29: What sort of challenges do you enjoy?

Answer:

The challenges you enjoy should demonstrate some sort of initiative or growth potential on your part, and should also be in line with your career objectives. Employers will evaluate consistency here, as they analyze critically how the challenges you look forward to are related to your ultimate goals.

30: Tell me about a time you were embarrassed. How did you

handle it?

Answer:

No one wants to bring up times they were embarrassed in a job interview, and it's probably best to avoid an anecdote here. However, don't shy away from offering a brief synopsis, followed by a display of your ability to laugh it off. Show the interviewer that it was not an event that impacted you significantly.

31: What is your greatest weakness?

Answer:

This is another one of the most popular questions asked in job interviews, so you should be prepared with an answer already. Try to come up with a weakness that you have that can actually be a strength in an alternate setting – such as, "I'm very detail-oriented and like to ensure that things are done correctly, so I sometimes have difficulty in delegating tasks to others." However, don't try to mask obvious weaknesses – if you have little practical experience in the field, mention that you're looking forward to great opportunities to further your knowledge.

32: What are the three best adjectives to describe you in a work setting?

Answer:

While these three adjectives probably already appear somewhere on your resume, don't be afraid to use them again in order to highlight your best qualities. This is a chance for you to sell yourself to the interviewer, and to point out traits you possess that other candidates do not. Use the most specific and accurate words you can think of, and elaborate shortly on how you embody each.

33: What are the three best adjectives to describe you in your personal life?

Answer:

Ideally, the three adjectives that describe you in your personal life should be similar to the adjectives that describe you in your professional life. Employers appreciate consistency, and while they may be understanding of you having an alternate personality outside of the office, it's best if you employ similar principles in your actions both on and off the clock.

34: What type of worker are you?

Answer:

This is an opportunity for you to highlight some of your greatest assets. Characterize some of your talents such as dedicated, self-motivated, detail-oriented, passionate, hard-working, analytical, or customer service focused. Stay away from your weaker qualities here, and remain on the target of all the wonderful things that you can bring to the company.

35: Tell me about your happiest day at work.

Answer:

Your happiest day at work should include one of your greatest professional successes, and how it made you feel. Stay focused on what you accomplished, and be sure to elaborate on how rewarding or satisfying the achievement was for you.

36: Tell me about your worst day at work.

Answer:

It may have been the worst day ever because of all the mistakes you made, or because you'd just had a huge argument with your best friend, but make sure to keep this answer professionally focused. Try to use an example in which something uncontrollable happened in the workplace (such as an important member of a team quit unexpectedly, which ruined your team's meeting with a client), and focus on the frustration of not being in control of the situation. Keep this answer brief, and be sure to end with a reflection on what you learned from the day.

37: What are you passionate about?

Answer:

Keep this answer professionally-focused where possible, but it may also be appropriate to discuss personal issues you are passionate about as well (such as the environment or volunteering at a soup kitchen). Stick to issues that are non-controversial, and allow your passion to shine through as you explain what inspires you about the topic and how you stay actively engaged in it. Additionally, if you choose a personal passion, make sure it is one that does not detract from your availability to work or to be productive.

38: What is the piece of criticism you receive most often?

Answer:

An honest, candid answer to this question can greatly impress an interviewer (when, of course, it is coupled with an explanation of what you're doing to improve), but make sure the criticism is something minimal or unrelated to your career.

39: What type of work environment do you succeed the most in?

Answer:

Be sure to research the company and the specific position before heading into the interview. Tailor your response to fit the job you'd be working in, and explain why you enjoy that type of environment over others. However, it's also extremely important to be adaptable, so remain flexible to other environments as well.

40: Are you an emotional person?

Answer:

It's best to focus on your positive emotions – passion, happiness, motivations – and to stay away from other extreme emotions that may cause you to appear unbalanced. While you want to display your excitement for the job, be sure to remain level-headed and cool at all times, so that the interviewer knows you're not the type of person who lets emotions take you over and get in the way of your work.

41: What is the best way for a company to advertise?

Answer:

If you're going for a position in any career other than marketing, this question is probably intended to demonstrate your ability to think critically and to provide reflective support for your answers. As such, the particular method you choose is not so important as why you've chosen it. For example, word of mouth advertising is important because customers will inherently trust the source, and social media advertising is important as it reaches new customers quickly and cheaply.

42: Is it better to gain a new customer or to keep an old one?

Answer:

In almost every case, it is better to keep an old customer, and it's important that you are able to articulate why this is. First, new customers generally cost companies more than retaining old ones does, and new customers are more likely to switch to a different company. Additionally, keeping old customers is a great way to provide a stable backbone for the company, as well as to also gain new customers as they are likely to recommend your company to friends.

43: What is the best way to win clients from competitors?

Answer:

There are many schools of thought on the best way to win clients from competitors, and unless you know that your interviewer adheres to a specific thought or practice, it's best to keep this question general. Rather than using absolute language, focus on the benefits of one or two strategies and show a clear, critical understanding of how these ways can succeed in a practical application.

44: How do you feel about companies monitoring internet usage?

Answer:

Generally speaking, most companies will monitor some degree of internet usage over their employees – and during an interview is not the best time to rebel against this practice. Instead, focus on positive aspects such as the way it can lead to increased productivity for some employees who may be easily lost in the world of resourceful information available to them.

45: What is your first impression of our company?

Answer:

Obviously, this should be a positive answer! Pick out a couple key components of the company's message or goals that you especially identify with or that pertain to your experience, and discuss why you believe these missions are so important.

46: Tell me about your personal philosophy on business.

Answer:

Your personal philosophy on business should be well-thought out, and in line with the missions and objectives of the company. Stay focused on positive aspects such as the service it can provide, and the lessons people gain in business, and offer insight as to where your philosophy has come from.

47: What's most important in a business model: sales, customer service, marketing, management, etc.?

Answer:

For many positions, it may be a good strategy to tailor this answer to the type of field you're working in, and to explain why that aspect of business is key. However, by explaining that each aspect is integral to the function as a whole, you can display a greater sense of business savvy to the interviewer and may stand out in his or her mind as a particularly aware candidate.

48: How do you keep up with news and emerging trends in the

field?

Answer:

The interviewer wants to see that you are aware of what's currently going on in your field. It is important that your education does not stop after college, and the most successful candidates will have a list of resources they regularly turn to already in place, so that they may stay aware and engaged in developing trends.

49: Would you have a problem adhering to company policies on social media?

Answer:

Social media concerns in the workplace have become a greater issue, and many companies now outline policies for the use of social media. Interviewers will want to be assured that you won't have a problem adhering to company standards, and that you will maintain a consistent, professional image both in the office and online.

50: Tell me about one of the greatest problems facing *X industry* today.

Answer:

If you're involved in your career field, and spend time on your own studying trends and new developments, you should be able to display an awareness of both problems and potential solutions coming up in the industry. Research some of the latest news before heading into the interview, and be prepared to discuss current events thoroughly.

51: What do you think it takes to be successful in our company?

Answer:

Research the company prior to the interview. Be aware of the company's mission and main objectives, as well as some of the biggest names in the company, and also keep in mind how they achieved success. Keep your answer focused on specific objectives you could reach in order to help the company achieve its goals.

52: What is your favorite part of working in this career field?

Answer:

This question is an opportunity to discuss some of your favorite aspects of the job, and to highlight why you are a great candidate for the particular position. Choose elements of the work you enjoy that are related to what you would do if hired for the position. Remember to remain enthusiastic and excited for the opportunities you could attain in the job.

53: What do you see happening to your career in the next 10 years?

Answer:

If you're plugged in to what's happening in your career now, and are making an effort to stay abreast of emerging trends in your field, you should be able to offer the interviewer several predictions as to where your career or field may be heading. This insight and level of awareness shows a level of dedication and interest that is important to employers.

54: Describe a time when you communicated a difficult or

complicated idea to a coworker.

Answer:

Start by explaining the idea briefly to the interviewer, and then give an overview of why it was necessary to break it down further to the coworker. Finally, explain the idea in succinct steps, so the interviewer can see your communication abilities and skill in simplification.

55: What situations do you find it difficult to communicate in?

Answer:

Even great communicators will often find particular situations that are more difficult to communicate effectively in, so don't be afraid to answer this question honestly. Be sure to explain why the particular situation you name is difficult for you, and try to choose an uncommon answer such as language barrier or in time of hardship, rather than a situation such as speaking to someone of higher authority.

56: What are the key components of good communication?

Answer:

Some of the components of good communication include an environment that is free from distractions, feedback from the listener, and revision or clarification from the speaker when necessary. Refer to basic communication models where necessary, and offer to go through a role-play sample with the interviewer in order to show your skills.

57: Tell me about a time when you solved a problem through communication.

Answer:

Solving problems through communication is key in the business world, so choose a specific situation from your previous job in which you navigated a messy situation by communicating effectively through the conflict. Explain the basis of the situation, as well as the communication steps you took, and end with a discussion of why communicating through the problem was so important to its resolution.

58: Tell me about a time when you had a dispute with another employee. How did you resolve the situation?

Answer:

Make sure to use a specific instance, and explain step-by-step the scenario, what you did to handle it, and how it was finally resolved. The middle step, how you handled the dispute, is clearly the most definitive – describe the types of communication you used, and how you used compromise to reach a decision. Conflict resolution is an important skill for any employee to have, and is one that interviewers will search for to determine both how likely you are to be involved in disputes, and how likely they are to be forced to become involved in the dispute if one arises.

59: Do you build relationships quickly with people, or take more time to get to know them?

Answer:

Either of these options can display good qualities, so determine which style is more applicable to you. Emphasize the steps you take in relationship-building over the particular style, and summarize briefly why this works best for you.

60: Describe a time when you had to work through office politics to solve a problem.

Answer:

Try to focus on the positives in this question, so that you can use the situation to your advantage. Don't portray your previous employer negatively, and instead use a minimal instance (such as paperwork or a single individual), to highlight how you worked through a specific instance resourcefully. Give examples of communication skills or problem-solving you used in order to achieve a resolution.

61: Tell me about a time when you persuaded others to take on a difficult task?

Answer:

This question is an opportunity to highlight both your leadership and communication skills. While the specific situation itself is important to offer as background, focus on how you were able to persuade the others, and what tactics worked the best.

62: Tell me about a time when you successfully persuaded a group to accept your proposal.

Answer:

This question is designed to determine your resourcefulness and your communication skills. Explain the ways in which you took into account different perspectives within the group, and created a presentation that would be appealing and convincing to all members. Additionally, you can pump up the proposal itself by offering details about it that show how well-executed it was.

63: Tell me about a time when you had a problem with another person, that, in hindsight, you wished you had handled differently.

Answer:

The key to this question is to show your capabilities of reflection and your learning process. Explain the situation, how you handled it at the time, what the outcome of the situation was, and finally, how you would handle it now. Most importantly, tell the interviewer why you would handle it differently now – did your previous solution create stress on the relationship with the other person, or do you wish that you had stood up more for what you wanted? While you shouldn't elaborate on how poorly you handled the situation before, the most important thing is to show that you've grown and reached a deeper level of understanding as a result of the conflict.

64: Tell me about a time when you negotiated a conflict between other employees.

Answer:

An especially important question for those interviewing for a supervisory role – begin with a specific situation, and explain how you communicated effectively to each individual. For example, did you introduce a compromise? Did you make an executive decision? Or, did you perform as a mediator and encourage the employees to reach a conclusion on their own?

65: Why would your skills be a good match with *X objective* of our company?

Answer:

If you've researched the company before the interview, answering this question should be no problem. Determine several of the company's main objectives, and explain how specific skills that you have are conducive to them. Also, think about ways that your experience and skills can translate to helping the company expand upon these objectives, and to reach further goals. If your old company had a similar objective, give a specific example of how you helped the company to meet it.

66: What do you think this job entails?

Answer:

Make sure you've researched the position well before heading into the interview. Read any and all job descriptions you can find (at best, directly from the employer's website or job posting), and make note of key duties, responsibilities, and experience required. Few things are less impressive to an interviewer than a candidate who has no idea what sort of job they're actually being interviewed for.

67: Is there anything else about the job or company you'd like to know?

Answer:

If you have learned about the company beforehand, this is a great opportunity to show that you put in the effort to study before the interview. Ask questions about the company's mission in relation to current industry trends, and engage the interviewer in interesting, relevant conversation. Additionally, clear up anything else you need to know about the specific position before leaving – so that if the interviewer calls with an offer, you'll be prepared to answer.

68: Are you the best candidate for this position?

Answer:

Yes! Offer specific details about what makes you qualified for this position, and be sure to discuss (and show) your unbridled passion and enthusiasm for the new opportunity, the job, and the company.

69: How did you prepare for this interview?

Answer:

The key part of this question is to make sure that you have prepared! Be sure that you've researched the company, their objectives, and their services prior to the interview, and know as much about the specific position as you possibly can. It's also helpful to learn about the company's history and key players in the current organization.

70: If you were hired here, what would you do on your first day?

Answer:

While many people will answer this question in a boring fashion, going through the standard first day procedures, this question is actually a great chance for you to show the interviewer why you will make a great hire. In addition to things like going through training or orientation, emphasize how much you would enjoy meeting your supervisors and coworkers, or how you would spend a lot of the day asking questions and taking in all of your new surroundings.

71: Have you viewed our company's website?

Answer:

Clearly, you should have viewed the company's website and done some preliminary research on them before coming to the interview. If for some reason you did not, do not say that you did, as the interviewer may reveal you by asking a specific question about it. If you did look at the company's website, this is an appropriate time to bring up something you saw there that was of particular interest to you, or a value that you especially supported.

72: How does X *experience* on your resume relate to this position?

Answer:

Many applicants will have some bit of experience on their resume that does not clearly translate to the specific job in question. However, be prepared to be asked about this type of seemingly-irrelevant experience, and have a response prepared that takes into account similar skill sets or training that the two may share.

73: Why do you want this position?

Answer:

Keep this answer focused positively on aspects of this specific job that will allow you to further your skills, offer new experience, or that will be an opportunity for you to do something that you particularly enjoy. Don't tell the interviewer that you've been looking for a job for a long time, or that the pay is very appealing, or you will appear unmotivated and opportunistic.

74: How is your background relevant to this position?

Answer:

Ideally, this should be obvious from your resume. However, in instances where your experience is more loosely-related to the position, make sure that you've researched the job and company well before the interview. That way, you can intelligently relate the experience and skills that you do have, to similar skills that would be needed in the new position. Explain specifically how your skills will translate, and use words to describe your background such as "preparation" and "learning." Your prospective position should be described as an "opportunity" and a chance for "growth and development."

75: How do you feel about *X mission* of our company?

Answer:

It's important to have researched the company prior to the interview – and if you've done so, this question won't catch you off guard. The best answer is one that is simple, to the point, and shows knowledge of the mission at hand. Offer a few short statements as to why you believe in the mission's importance, and note that you would be interested in the chance to work with a company that supports it.

INDEX

Advanced C++ Interview Questions

General Concepts

22: Do you think the following code will serve its purpose? Explain your answer.

23: What is the purpose of the stream manipulator 'setw'? Which header file should be included for using the stream manipulators in the program?

24: Predict the output:

25: What is the purpose of the rand() function? Why is srand() used?

26: Illustrate the use of srand() by providing few statements.

27: How can you limit the value of random numbers generated in the range of 1 through 100?

28: How will you get the content from the header?

29: How does the statement "cout" works?

30: How will you prevent the console window from closing once it finished the execution?

31: What is called undeclared variable?

32: How does the function of "=" and "==" differs?

33: How much space will be occupied by the data types "char,int,double and float"?

34: How do the local and global variables differs in scope?

35: What are the ways to initialize the variables?

36: What is the purpose of "wide character"?

37: What is the use of "define preprocessor"?

38: What are the ways to define a constant in C++?

39: What is the purpose of comma (,) operator in C++?

40: What is the output of the expression "3 + 8 / 4"? 5 or 2.6?

41: How are the I/O operations performed in C++?

42: How do you get a string as input?

43: What are the two error streams in C++ and what is the difference between them?

Control Statements and Decision Making

44: How do you write an infinite loop in C++ using the for statement?

45: Assuming x = 20, y = 15; what would be the value stored in 'a' after the following statement is executed:

46: Predict the output:

47: Predict the output:

48: Write an 'if' statement that checks the value of variable 'age' to determine whether it is in the range of 18 through 65 and displays 'Acceptable age', when the condition is fulfilled.

49: When do you use a conditional operator (?:) ?

50: Write a statement using conditional operator that assigns 0 to x, if y is greater than 10, otherwise assigns 1 to x.

51: Rewrite the following expression, using an if-else statement:

52: Can you change the following if-else statement block into a switch statement?

53: Predict the output:

54: Predict the output:

55: Predict the output:

56: Convert the following if-else statement into a conditional expression:

57: Write a for-loop statement that will print the numbers 1 through 10, but skip the number 5.

58: A program asks for a number in the range of 1 through 100. Write a simple while loop for input validation.

Functions and Recursion

59: What's wrong with the following function?

60: What is a function prototype? Write a prototype for a function add (), which takes the reference to two integer variables and returns another integer

61: What is the difference between a local variable and a global variable?

62: Why global variables should not be preferred?

63: What is a global constant?

64: What are the five storage class specifiers in C++?

65: What does the function fmod (x, y) return?

66: What is the difference between the function ceil(x) and the function floor(x)?

67: Predict the output:

68: Predict the output:

69: Is it right to call the function doubleNum of the last question as -- doubleNum(a + 5) ?

70: What is function overloading?

71: Can the overloaded function have different return types?

72: What is a function template? How do you define a function template?

73: What is a 'stub'? What is a 'driver'? When are they used?

74: What does the following function achieve?

Arrays and Vectors

75: How much memory should be occupied by the array: char array [25]?

76: What's wrong with the following code snippet?

77: Is the following array initialization valid?

78: Is it possible to define an array without specifying its size?

79: What would be printed?

80: How can you prevent a function to modify the contents of an array that is passed to it as an argument?

81: How do you define a vector?

82: Which header file needs to be included to use vectors in your program?

83: Define a vector of 10 integers.

84: Can you initialize the elements of a vector while defining?

85: Is it possible to initialize a vector with another vector without element-wise assignment? Is it possible to do the same with an array?

86: What happens when you add a value to a vector that is already full?

87: What is wrong with the following assignment?

88: How can you determine the size of a vector?

89: How do you remove the last element from a vector?

90: How can you clear the contents of a vector completely?

91: What is the purpose of the vector member function empty() ?

92: How do you retrieve a value stored at a particular element in the vector?

Pointers

93: Can you use delete this?

94: What are pointers?

95: Predict the output:

96: Predict the output:

97: Predict the output:

98: Predict the output:

99: Is it possible to compare pointers using the C++ relational operators?

100: What is the difference between pointers to constant data and constant pointers?

101: Why could you declare a pointer parameter as a constant pointer?

102: What is the purpose of the new operator?

103: What is the purpose of the delete operator?

104: What is a function pointer?

105: Declare a function pointer that will take two integer parameter and return a Boolean value.

Control Structures, Array and Pointers

106: What are the control statements used in C++?

107: What is the function of continue and break?

108: What will happen if you pass a variable var1 as an argument to a function(arg1) from main() and make changes to the variable within the called function ?

109: Give an example for normal function call and call by reference.

110: How will you assign a default value for last parameter in a function?

111: How will you store the elements of the same type in a continuous memory location?

112: How much memory space will be allocated for the array of integer type with length 4?

113: How will you display the output with a particular space to be filled by specified amount?

114: How will you get the address of an array variable?

115: What are the ways of passing an array as an argument?

Object Oriented Programming and Classes

which one calls assignment operator?

142: What are Virtual functions?

143: Can you define a Virtual Copy Constructor?

144: What is an 'object' in object oriented programming?

145: What is 'encapsulation'?

146: What is 'data hiding'?

147: What is the default access of a class?

148: When do you use the const keyword with member functions?

149: Can you declare constructors and destructors as const?

150: What is a friend function? What are the friend classes?

151: Class A is a friend of class B. Can class B access the members of class A?

152: What is this pointer?

153: The memory used up by this pointer is not counted in the size of the object. Why is it so?

154: Can friend functions be overloaded?

155: What are the static data members of a class?

156: Explain the register storage class.

157: Do you agree with the statement: The static member functions do not have a 'this' pointer. Why?

158: What is a constructor?

159: What is a destructor?

160: Predict the output:

161: What is the difference between the 'Student' structure and the 'Student' class?

162: Predict the output:

163: What is a copy constructor?

164: Which operators cannot be overloaded?

165: How does C++ differentiate between overloaded postfix operators and prefix operators?

166: Consider the following class student:

167: Write a constructor for the class student described above, which will take two parameters, a string for name and an int for no_of_tests and assign a default score of 0.0 to all the tests.

168: Write a destructor for the class student described above.

169: How do you overload an operator?

170: Why should an overloaded operator always be a non-static function?

171: Can you change the precedence and associativity of an operator by overloading it?

172: Can you change the number of operands an operator works on by overloading it?

173: Can you create a new operator by operator overloading?

174: What is wrong with the statement?

Inheritance, Polymorphism and Virtual Functions

175: Explain Conditional Compilation.

176: Explain when # is used and ## is used in C++.

177: What is inheritance?

178: Is it possible for a base class to call a member function of a derived class?

179: What is the basic difference between inheritance and composition?

180: Who can access the protected members of a base class?

181: Can a derived class access the private members of the base class?

182: What is the default access specification of a base class?

183: Predict the output:

184: What is polymorphism?

185: How is polymorphism implemented in C++?

186: What is the difference between redefining a base class function and overloading a base class function?

187: How is static binding different from dynamic binding?

188: Pointers to a base class may be assigned the address of a derived class object. Does it work in reverse?

189: How can you make a derived class object pointer point to a base class object?

190: When and why should you declare a destructor as virtual?

191: What is an abstract base class?

192: What is the characteristic of a pure virtual function?

193: How do you declare a pure virtual function?

194: What is wrong in the following code?

195: What is multiple Inheritance?

196: We cannot instantiate objects of an abstract base class. Can we declare pointers to objects of an abstract class?

197: What is the purpose of the dynamic_cast operator?

198: What is the purpose of the typeid operator?

199: What is the importance of the dynamic_cast and the typeid operators with respect to polymorphism?

Exceptions and Exception Handling

200: What is an exception?

201: What is the purpose of exception handling?

202: What is a 'try' block?

203: How are the exceptions caught?

204: What is a 'throw point'?

205: What happens when an exception is caught?

206: What is 'rethrowing' an exception?

207: What do you mean by 'unwinding the stack' in reference with exception handling?

208: What happens if the new operator fails?

209: What is an exception specification?

210: What happens when a function does not have an exception specification?

Class Template and Standard Template Library (STL)

211: Explain Signal Handling.

212: How are STL and Object Class Library related?

213: What is a class template?

214: What does the Standard Template Library contain?

215: What are the most important data structures defined in STL?

216: What is a container?

217: What is an iterator?

218: What is the difference between a sequential container and an associative container?

219: What are the sequential containers present in STL?

220: What are the associative containers present in STL?

221: What is the difference between the set and multiset data structures?

222: What is the difference between map and multimap data structures?

223: Assume that you have a vector object 'vect' of integers. Write a for loop to access its elements using an iterator.

224: Which algorithm randomly shuffles the elements in a container?

Functions, Class and Template

225: What is the way to bind the functions and variables in a single structure?

226: When a function or variable is defined with a private access specifier, what is the accessibility of that function?

227: How will you create a function definition of a class outside of that class?

228: How will you initialize an object?

229: How will you clear the dynamically allocated memory?

230: Can a constructor be overloaded?

231: How will you create an object to call a overloaded constructor function?

232: How will you pass an object as argument to a function?

233: Give an example for creating a pointer to class.

234: Give an example for polymorphism.

235: What will happen if the super class function's access specifier is protected and you are trying to override this function in sub class with 'private' access specifier?

236: What will happen if the object of sub class is created and assigned to its super class reference variable as stated below?

237: Give an example for function overriding.

238: How will you overload an operator?

239: How will you declare and initialize a static member?

240: Consider a template class that contains one function. When an object of particular type is created, how will you implement the template that should contain different method?

241: How will you access the variable declared inside the namespace?

242: How will you the use the variable in namespace without using "::"

243: What are the ways to do type casting?

244: How will you use an existing file for an output operation?

Stream Input Output

245: C++ offers type-safe I/O – explain.

246: How can you use the stream insertion operator (<<) and the stream extraction operator (>>) on user-defined data type?

247: How can the stream extraction operator >> and the stream insertion operator << work upon all types of data?

248: How can you change the base in which integers output?

249: Predict the output:

250: What is the purpose of the stream manipulator scientific?

251: What is the purpose of the stream manipulator boolalpha?

File Processing

252: Which file access flag would you use if you want all output to be written to the end of an existing file?

253: What is the specialty of the fstream data type that the ifstream and ofstream data types do not have?

254: Assume that the file info.txt already exists, and the following statement executes. What happens to the file?

255: Should file stream objects be passed to functions by value or by reference? Why?

256: Explain ios::hardfail, the file stream object bit.

257: When is a file stream object's ios::eofbit bit set? Which member function reports the state of this bit?

258: How do you read the contents of a text file that contains whitespace characters as part of its data?

259: What are the arguments to be passed to a file stream object's write member function?

260: What are the arguments to be passed to a file stream object's read member function?

261: What type cast do you use to convert a pointer from one type to another?

262: What is the difference between the seekg and seekp member functions?

263: How do you get the byte number of a file's current read position? How do you get the byte number of a file's current write position?

264: How do you determine the number of bytes that a file contains?

265: Write a statement that defines a file stream object named students. The object will be used for both output and input to and from a file.

266: Write a code snippet that defines a file stream object named employees. The file should be opened for both input and output in binary mode. If the file open operation fails, it should display an error message.

267: What does the following code achieve?

268: The data File file stream object is used to sequentially access data. The program has already read to the end of the file. Write code that rewinds the file.

Miscellaneous

269: Explain the ? : Operator.

270: Explain stack and heap in C++.

271: How is dynamic memory allocation done in C++ efficiently?

272: Explain Multithreading in C++.

273: Explain CGI.

274: Why CGI is a better choice than other scripting languages?

HR Questions

1: Tell me about a time when you didn't meet a deadline.

2: How do you eliminate distractions while working?

3: Tell me about a time when you worked in a position with a weekly or monthly quota to meet. How often were you successful?

4: Tell me about a time when you met a tough deadline, and how you were able to complete it.

5: How do you stay organized when you have multiple projects on your plate?

6: How much time during your work day do you spend on "auto-pilot?"

7: How do you handle deadlines?

8: Tell me about your personal problem-solving process.

9: What sort of things at work can make you stressed?

10: What do you look like when you are stressed about something? How do you solve it?

11: Can you multi-task?

12: How many hours per week do you work?

13: How many times per day do you check your email?

14: What has been your biggest success?

15: What motivates you?

16: What do you do when you lose motivation?

17: What do you like to do in your free time?

18: What sets you apart from other workers?

19: Why are you the best candidate for that position?

20: What does it take to be successful?

21: What would be the biggest challenge in this position for you?

22: Would you describe yourself as an introvert or an extrovert?

23: What are some positive character traits that you don't possess?

24: What is the greatest lesson you've ever learned?

25: Have you ever been in a situation where one of your strengths became a weakness in an alternate setting?

idea to a coworker.

55: What situations do you find it difficult to communicate in?

56: What are the key components of good communication?

57: Tell me about a time when you solved a problem through communication?

58: Tell me about a time when you had a dispute with another employee. How did you resolve the situation?

59: Do you build relationships quickly with people, or take more time to get to know them?

60: Describe a time when you had to work through office politics to solve a problem.

61: Tell me about a time when you persuaded others to take on a difficult task?

62: Tell me about a time when you successfully persuaded a group to accept your proposal.

63: Tell me about a time when you had a problem with another person, that, in hindsight, you wished you had handled differently.

64: Tell me about a time when you negotiated a conflict between other employees.

65: Why would your skills be a good match with X objective of our company?

66: What do you think this job entails?

67: Is there anything else about the job or company you'd like to know?

68: Are you the best candidate for this position?

69: How did you prepare for this interview?

70: If you were hired here, what would you do on your first day?

71: Have you viewed our company's website?

72: How does X experience on your resume relate to this position?

73: Why do you want this position?

74: How is your background relevant to this position?

75: How do you feel about X mission of our company?

Some of the following titles might also be handy:

1. .NET Interview Questions You'll Most Likely Be Asked
2. 200 Interview Questions You'll Most Likely Be Asked
3. Access VBA Programming Interview Questions You'll Most Likely Be Asked
4. Adobe ColdFusion Interview Questions You'll Most Likely Be Asked
5. Advanced C++ Interview Questions You'll Most Likely Be Asked
6. Advanced Excel Interview Questions You'll Most Likely Be Asked
7. Advanced JAVA Interview Questions You'll Most Likely Be Asked
8. Advanced SAS Interview Questions You'll Most Likely Be Asked
9. AJAX Interview Questions You'll Most Likely Be Asked
10. Algorithms Interview Questions You'll Most Likely Be Asked
11. Android Development Interview Questions You'll Most Likely Be Asked
12. Ant & Maven Interview Questions You'll Most Likely Be Asked
13. Apache Web Server Interview Questions You'll Most Likely Be Asked
14. Artificial Intelligence Interview Questions You'll Most Likely Be Asked
15. ASP.NET Interview Questions You'll Most Likely Be Asked
16. Automated Software Testing Interview Questions You'll Most Likely Be Asked
17. Base SAS Interview Questions You'll Most Likely Be Asked
18. BEA WebLogic Server Interview Questions You'll Most Likely Be Asked
19. C & C++ Interview Questions You'll Most Likely Be Asked
20. C# Interview Questions You'll Most Likely Be Asked
21. CCNA Interview Questions You'll Most Likely Be Asked
22. Cloud Computing Interview Questions You'll Most Likely Be Asked
23. Computer Architecture Interview Questions You'll Most Likely Be Asked
24. Computer Networks Interview Questions You'll Most Likely Be Asked
25. Core JAVA Interview Questions You'll Most Likely Be Asked
26. Data Structures & Algorithms Interview Questions You'll Most Likely Be Asked
27. EJB 3.0 Interview Questions You'll Most Likely Be Asked
28. Entity Framework Interview Questions You'll Most Likely Be Asked
29. Fedora & RHEL Interview Questions You'll Most Likely Be Asked
30. Hibernate, Spring & Struts Interview Questions You'll Most Likely Be Asked
31. HTML, XHTML and CSS Interview Questions You'll Most Likely Be Asked
32. HTML5 Interview Questions You'll Most Likely Be Asked
33. IBM WebSphere Application Server Interview Questions You'll Most Likely Be Asked
34. iOS SDK Interview Questions You'll Most Likely Be Asked
35. Java / J2EE Design Patterns Interview Questions You'll Most Likely Be Asked
36. Java / J2EE Interview Questions You'll Most Likely Be Asked
37. JavaScript Interview Questions You'll Most Likely Be Asked
38. JavaServer Faces Interview Questions You'll Most Likely Be Asked
39. JDBC Interview Questions You'll Most Likely Be Asked
40. jQuery Interview Questions You'll Most Likely Be Asked
41. JSP-Servlet Interview Questions You'll Most Likely Be Asked
42. JUnit Interview Questions You'll Most Likely Be Asked
43. Linux Interview Questions You'll Most Likely Be Asked
44. Linux System Administrator Interview Questions You'll Most Likely Be Asked
45. Mac OS X Lion Interview Questions You'll Most Likely Be Asked
46. Mac OS X Snow Leopard Interview Questions You'll Most Likely Be Asked
47. Microsoft Access Interview Questions You'll Most Likely Be Asked
48. Microsoft Powerpoint Interview Questions You'll Most Likely Be Asked
49. Microsoft Word Interview Questions You'll Most Likely Be Asked
50. MySQL Interview Questions You'll Most Likely Be Asked

51. Networking Interview Questions You'll Most Likely Be Asked
52. OOPS Interview Questions You'll Most Likely Be Asked
53. Operating Systems Interview Questions You'll Most Likely Be Asked
54. Oracle Database Administration Interview Questions You'll Most Likely Be Asked
55. Oracle E-Business Suite Interview Questions You'll Most Likely Be Asked
56. ORACLE PL/SQL Interview Questions You'll Most Likely Be Asked
57. Perl Programming Interview Questions You'll Most Likely Be Asked
58. PHP Interview Questions You'll Most Likely Be Asked
59. Python Interview Questions You'll Most Likely Be Asked
60. RESTful JAVA Web Services Interview Questions You'll Most Likely Be Asked
61. SAP HANA Interview Questions You'll Most Likely Be Asked
62. SAS Programming Guidelines Interview Questions You'll Most Likely Be Asked
63. Selenium Testing Tools Interview Questions You'll Most Likely Be Asked
64. Silverlight Interview Questions You'll Most Likely Be Asked
65. Software Repositories Interview Questions You'll Most Likely Be Asked
66. Software Testing Interview Questions You'll Most Likely Be Asked
67. SQL Server Interview Questions You'll Most Likely Be Asked
68. Tomcat Interview Questions You'll Most Likely Be Asked
69. UML Interview Questions You'll Most Likely Be Asked
70. Unix Interview Questions You'll Most Likely Be Asked
71. UNIX Shell Programming Interview Questions You'll Most Likely Be Asked
72. Windows Server 2008 R2 Interview Questions You'll Most Likely Be Asked
73. XLXP, XSLT, XPATH, XFORMS & XQuery Interview Questions You'll Most Likely Be Asked
74. XML Interview Questions You'll Most Likely Be Asked

For complete list visit

www.vibrantpublishers.com

CPSIA information can be obtained
at www.ICGtesting.com
Printed in the USA
LVHW080327130122
708310LV00022BA/3034